EARTH

The Ever-Changing Planet

About the cover: The picture on the cover does not show a real landscape. It was drawn to fit all of the following into one scene: mountains, hills, valleys, glaciers, islands, plains, cliffs, rivers, a delta, and the sea.

But look carefully. Can you also find waterfalls, icebergs, beaches, sand dunes, buttes, a cave, a stack, a sea arch, a spit, a geyser, a crater lake, a natural bridge, and a volcano with steam shooting out of it?

EARTH

THE EVER-CHANGING PLANET

BY **Donald M. Silver,** PH.D.

ILLUSTRATED BY **Patricia J. Wynne**

Random House  New York

For my mother
—*Patricia Jewell Wynne*

I wish to thank Melinda Luke and
Regina Kahney for their valuable
editorial suggestions about how to
reshape my view of planet Earth. I
greatly appreciated the enthusiastic
and enlightening comments provided
by Dr. Graham Wilson of Turnstone
Geological Services, Ltd., Toronto,
Ontario, and Jos. Trautwein's expert
design assistance. Once again, I am
grateful to Thomas L. Cathey for his
friendly criticism of my work.
—*Donald M. Silver*, Ph.D.

Key of Abbreviations
cm = centimeter (2.54 cm = 1 inch)
m = meter (0.3 m = 1 foot)
km = kilometer (1.6 km = 1 mile)
kph = kilometers per hour

BOOK DESIGN
Bentwood Studio / Jos. Trautwein

Library of Congress Cataloging-in-Publication Data
Silver, Donald M.
   Earth : The ever-changing planet / by Donald M. Silver ;
illustrated by Patricia J. Wynne.
      p. cm.— (The Random House library of knowl-
edge ; 9) Includes index.
   SUMMARY: An illustrated survey of the earth describing
how it was formed and including information on different
types of rock, weathering and erosion, the formation of
mountains, and plate tectonics.
   ISBN: 0–394–89195–3 (pbk.); 0–394–99195–8 (lib. bdg.)
   1. Geology—Juvenile literature. [1. Geology.] I. Wynne,
Patricia, ill. II. Title. III. Series. QE29.S49 1989
550—dc19 88–11331

Manufactured in the United States of America
1 2 3 4 5 6 7 8 9 0

CONTENTS

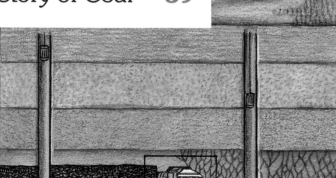

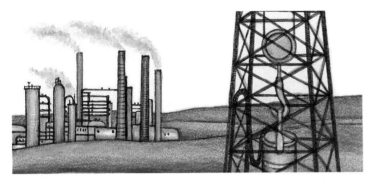

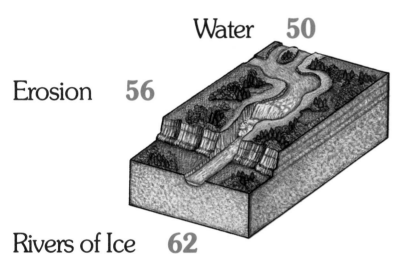
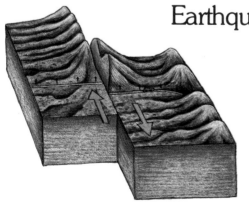

The Ever-Changing Planet

We live on the surface of the planet earth. It has vast oceans, deep canyons, and towering, snow-capped mountain peaks. It contains coal and uranium, diamonds and gold, copper and iron. Earth is the only place in the universe known to be alive with animals and plants.

Our world never stops changing. Mountains are being worn down into hills. Hidden from view, the ocean floors are slowly spreading apart. From moment to moment waves pound against rocky shores, rivers cut their way across continents, and glaciers creep down alpine slopes. On our world, volcanoes erupt, earthquakes destroy cities, and islands rise out of the sea.

Over billions of years great forces have shaped and reshaped the earth's surface. All around us there are clues to the ways these forces work. There are clues in the mud, clues in the rocks that sparkle in the sun. Under your house there may be fossils of dinosaurs that lived millions of years ago or shells that were once at the bottom of the ocean. There may be marks left by glaciers during the last ice age or lava rocks formed by an ancient volcano.

For centuries people have studied such clues, trying to unravel the mysteries of the earth's past. Since you were born, earth scientists, or geologists, have come closer than ever to understanding why our planet is so special.

The earth is a giant ball of rock whirling through space. It orbits the sun, spinning on its axis all the time. It is surrounded by a thick blanket of air called the atmosphere. The force of gravity pulls everything—even the atmosphere—toward the center of the earth. So much of the earth (71 percent) is covered by water that it is often called the water planet.

Scientists believe the earth has three main layers: the crust, the mantle, and the core. The crust is the outer layer of the earth. It is mostly lighter-weight rocks such as basalt and granite. It varies in thickness from 3 to 25 miles (5 to 40 kilometers), and it is thicker under the continents than it is under the oceans. Compare the earth to an apple, and the crust is almost as thin as the apple's skin.

Because we live on the surface of the crust, we know more about it than about the rest of our planet. Using special machines, people have drilled down into the crust to study what is inside the earth. The deeper they drill, the hotter it gets. One day

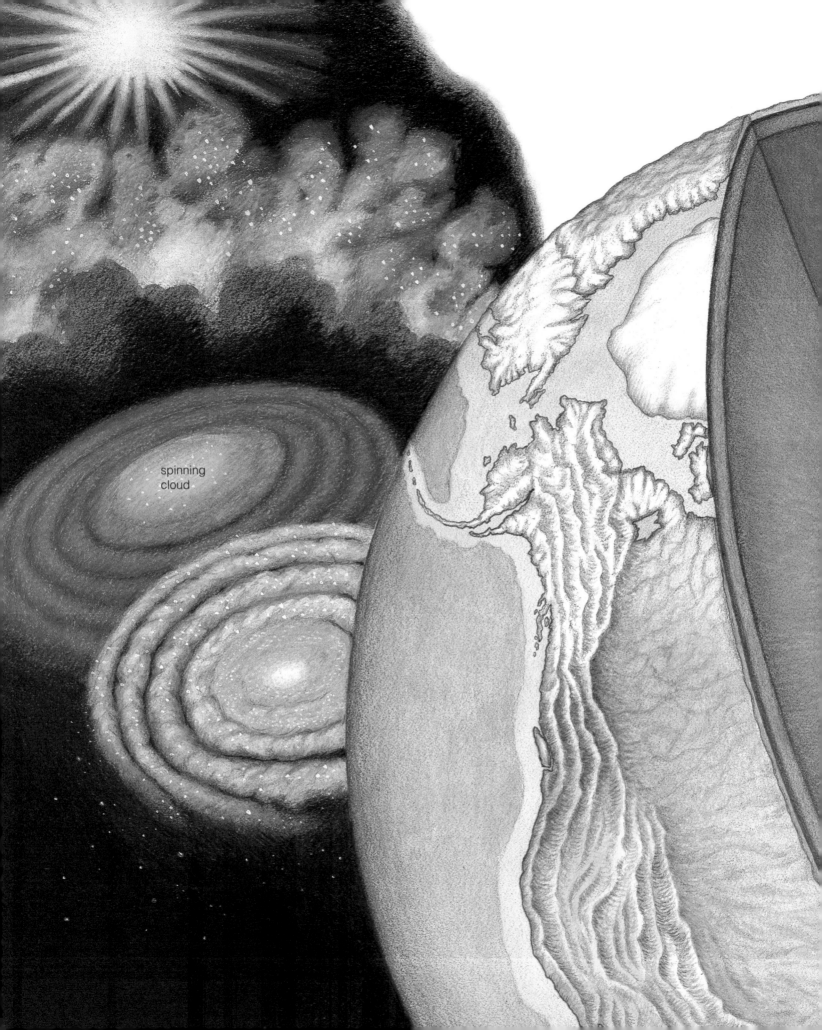

spinning
cloud

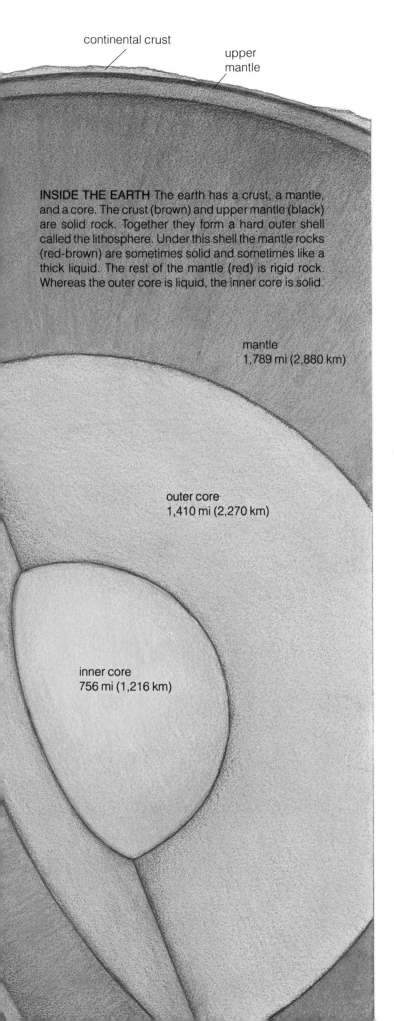

continental crust

upper mantle

INSIDE THE EARTH The earth has a crust, a mantle, and a core. The crust (brown) and upper mantle (black) are solid rock. Together they form a hard outer shell called the lithosphere. Under this shell the mantle rocks (red-brown) are sometimes solid and sometimes like a thick liquid. The rest of the mantle (red) is rigid rock. Whereas the outer core is liquid, the inner core is solid.

mantle
1,789 mi (2,880 km)

outer core
1,410 mi (2,270 km)

inner core
756 mi (1,216 km)

they will reach the bottom of the crust, where the rocks become denser. This boundary between the crust and the mantle is called the Moho, after scientist Andrija Mohorovicic, who discovered it.

The mantle is the middle layer of the earth. It is very hot and under a lot of pressure. Most geologists think that the top and bottom parts of the mantle are rigid rock. But between them, there are red-hot rocks that sometimes act like a solid and sometimes flow like a thick, mushy liquid.

Beneath the mantle is the third layer, or core. The core is larger than the planet Mars and under very great pressure. It is also the hottest part of the earth, almost as hot as the surface of the sun. Scientists think that the outer part of the core is a hot liquid rich in iron, whereas the inner core is mostly solid iron. If people ever were to reach the center of the earth, they would have to drill nearly 4,000 mi (6,400 km)—about the distance between Chicago and London.

The Story of the Earth

There are many different theories about how the earth formed. One is that about 15 billion years ago there was a gigantic explosion called the Big Bang. The explosion created huge clouds of hot gases and dust. Over billions of years the clouds cooled and started to spin, forming galaxies and stars. By about 5 billion years ago, the sun, 9 planets, and over 50 moons in our solar system had formed.

For some time after the Big Bang, the young planet earth was so hot that solid rocks melted. Out of the swirling, soupy mixture that formed, lightweight substances floated to the surface and started to cool. About 4.6 billion years ago, they hardened into the rocks of the earth's ancient crust. Above this crust there was no air or water, and no life.

By studying rocks and fossils, scientists have been able to divide the history of the earth into four eras. The eras are illustrated with pictures and a time line on the next ten pages. Eras are divided into periods. These are shown by different colors on the time line.

The Precambrian Era

The first era is called the Precambrian and is shown in pale yellow on the time line. The continents we live on today contain areas of Precambrian rock called

cratons. The oldest known rocks formed on the earth about 3.8 billion years ago and are found in Greenland. People are still searching for even older traces of the earth's past.

The Precambrian era lasted about 4 billion years—nearly 90 percent of the earth's history. Even so, very little is known about how our planet changed during this extremely long time. Scientists think that steam and hot gases from inside the earth escaped through volcanoes and slowly formed the first atmosphere and clouds. Enough rain eventually fell from the clouds to fill the oceans. About 3.5 billion years ago the first living things developed. They were simple bacteria made of just one cell and lived in the sea.

The Paleozoic Era

About 600 million years ago the Paleozoic era began. The word *paleozoic* comes from the Greek and means "ancient life." During the Paleozoic the earth's surface looked very different from the way it looks today (page 85). The Paleozoic is divided into six time periods. The first three are shown above: the Cambrian, the Ordovician, and the Silurian.

During the Cambrian volcanoes rose out of the sea,

spewing gases and lava. Thousands of different kinds of plants and animals evolved in the oceans. One-celled sea plants, called algae, made oxygen, which escaped into the air.

During the Ordovician and many times thereafter, large areas of continents were flooded by seawater. For millions of years the flooded land became sea floor where layers of sedimentary rocks (page 32) formed. Each time the shallow seas pulled back, they left the layered rocks on the continents.

By the end of the Ordovician, many ancient mountains had been worn away by the forces of weathering

The time line begins 4,600 million (4.6 billion) years ago, at the start of the Precambrian era. The illustration above each color on the line shows what the earth may have looked like during that time. MYA means "million years ago."

Most of the earth's history took place during the Precambrian era. Until the Ordovician period there were no bony animals and until the Silurian period no land plants or animals. Some of the primitive animals shown are **(a)** ancient sea pen, **(b)** ancient worm, **(c)** ancient jellyfish, **(d)** ancient sponge, **(e)** ancient brachiopod, **(f)** hallucigenia, **(g)** trilobite, **(h)** ancient crustacean, **(i)** ancient crinoid, **(j)** opabinia, **(k)** graptolite, **(l)** ancient coral, **(m)** ancient ostracod, **(n)** ancient snail, **(o)** nautiloid, **(p)** eurypterus, **(q)** didymograptus, **(r)** ancient fish.

(page 26) and erosion (page 56). But during the Silurian, a new surge of mountain building began.

These mountains too were worn away over hundreds of millions of years.

Throughout the past the climate has often changed on many parts of the earth's surface. During the Devonian, as in many other periods, there were times when it was very cold and times when it was very hot. During the cold times glaciers formed and moved over the land. During the hot, dry times glaciers melted, rivers and lakes dried up, and deserts became more common. In some places seawater evaporated from flooded lands, leaving behind layers of salt.

About 345 million years ago the Carboniferous period began. Great swampy forests grew in the warm, humid climate. When the forest plants died, many fell into the swampy waters. Over millions of years these dead plants became vast deposits of coal that are still being mined today.

The animal world changed during the 65 million years of the Carboniferous. Amphibians crawled out of the waters, and insects flew in the air. Reptiles, the first bony land animals, evolved.

The last period of the Paleozoic era was the Per-

12

mian. In many places it was a time of earthquakes and erupting volcanoes. It was also a time of mountain building, when majestic mountain ranges were pushed up high into the sky. Today's worn-down Appalachian and Ural mountains were as spectacular during the Permian as some mountains are today.

By the end of the Permian, a great change had taken place on the surface of the earth. Thousands of species of plants and animals had died out. No one knows why some living things became extinct while others survived. Whatever the reasons, the stage was set for a new era to begin.

During the Devonian period, giant fishes swam in the sea and the first amphibians moved out of water onto land. Many different kinds of plants grew in swampy forests during the Carboniferous period. Some of the animals shown are (a) ancient crinoid; (b) ancient coral, (c) bothriolepis, (d) nautiloid, (e) hemicyclapsis, (f) ancient sea star, (g) ancient brachiopod, (h) dinichtys, (i) trilobite, (j) pteraspis, (k) cladoselache, (l) ichthyostega, (m) crossopterygian, (n) giant dragonfly, (o) cockroach, (p) eogyrinus, (q) hylonomus, (r) ancient arachnid.

The Mesozoic Era

About 225 million years ago, the Mesozoic era began (*meso* means "middle"; *zoic* means "life"). It is sometimes called the Age of Reptiles, because dinosaurs and other giant reptiles evolved then and ruled the land, sea, and air. This era, which lasted 160 million years, is divided into the Triassic, Jurassic, and Cretaceous periods.

The earth's first dinosaurs, crocodiles, and mammals lived in the warm, dry Triassic climate. Around them many mountains continued to be worn down, and lava poured out of active volcanoes.

Dinosaurs of all sizes roamed the warm earth during the Jurassic. Herds of huge brontosauruses tramped past thick forests, still lakes, and winding rivers in search of food. Above broad plains, where fierce meat-eating dinosaurs preyed on plant eaters, ancient mountains rose. And while giant sea reptiles devoured fishes and squids, the first birds joined the flying reptiles in the air.

The last dinosaurs lived during the Cretaceous, the long, final period of the Mesozoic. Ferocious *Tyrannosaurus rex*, horned triceratopses, and duck-billed

hadrosaurs fed and fought to survive. Nearby, the first flowering plants grew out of the earth's fertile soil.

From the air, land, and sea the ruling reptiles witnessed the building of two great mountain chains—the Rockies and the Andes. Far away, at the bottom of the Atlantic and other oceans, underwater volcanoes continuously spewed out lava.

By the end of the Mesozoic all the dinosaurs had died out. So had all the flying reptiles, giant swimming reptiles, and many birds, mammals, and plants. What happened on the earth to cause such extinction? No one yet knows, but the Age of Reptiles was over.

The Permian was the last period of the Paleozoic era. It was followed by the Mesozoic era, when dinosaurs and other giant reptiles ruled the earth. Some of the animals shown are **(a)** edaphosaurus, **(b)** dimetrodon, **(c)** eryops, **(d)** plateosaurus, **(e)** saltopus, **(f)** saltoposuchus, **(g)** archaeopteryx, **(h)** rhamphoryhnchus, **(i)** allosaurus, **(j)** stegosaurus, **(k)** apatosaurus, **(l)** triceratops, **(m)** ankylosaurus, **(n)** ornithomimus, **(o)** tyrannosaurus, **(p)** anatosaurus.

15

TERTIARY

The Cenozoic Era

About 65 million years ago the era we are living in began. It is called the Cenozoic, which means "modern life." The Cenozoic is divided into the Tertiary and Quaternary periods—the time when the earth's surface gradually took on the shape it has today.

Mountains rose all over the Tertiary world. The old Rockies, Sierra Nevada, and Andes were pushed even higher, while the newborn Alps and Himalayas were thrust skyward, creating the tallest peaks on our planet. Tremendous earthquakes cracked the earth's crust deeply, and the lava that gushed out of volcanoes spread over land where people in Idaho, Oregon, and Washington live today. The huge Grand Canyon, which now awes visitors, was no canyon at all during the Tertiary—just a flat plain.

From the time that the dinosaurs completely disappeared, mammals dominated the earth. Mammals were very different from other animals. They grew hair or fur and produced milk to feed to their young. From mice to cats, horses to monkeys, most kinds of mammals we see today evolved on the Tertiary world. So did many giant mammals we will never see because

TERTIARY   **2 MYA**

they are now extinct.

By the end of the Tertiary, two major changes had taken place on earth. The first was the evolution of a new kind of hunting mammal—the human being. The second was the cooling of the climate that led to the great Ice Age.

The great Ice Age took place during the Quaternary period, which began about 2 million years ago. There had been ice ages before it, but none that so greatly affected the world we live on.

During the great Ice Age, massive sheets of glacial ice formed and spread over much of Europe, Asia, and

The Tertiary period began about 65 million years ago. It was a time of mountain building, earthquakes, and erupting volcanoes. New kinds of mammals evolved and dominated the land. By the end of the Tertiary the first human beings appeared and the climate cooled. Some of the animals shown are (a) opossum, (b) planetotherium, (c) pantolambda, (d) palaeoryctes, (e) plesiadapis, (f) machaeroides, (g) uintatherum, (h) palaeosyops, (i) orohippus, (j) tetonius, (k) metacheiromys, (l) hyrachyus, (m) cainotherium, (n) brontotherium, (o) patriofelis, (p) parahippus, (q) moropus, (r) poebrotherium, (s) pseudocynodictis, (t) syndyoceras, (u) deinotherium, (v) teleoceras, (w) merycodus, (x) megatylopus, (y) osteoborus, (z) epigaulus.

17

North America. The moving ice blanketed mountains, choked rivers, filled valleys, and flattened forests. In some places the ice was 3 mi (4.8 km) thick and the crust sank under its weight. So much of the earth's water was locked up as ice that oceans shrank in size. Continents grew larger as more and more land was exposed.

For about 250,000 years the cold climate kept much of the earth's surface under ice. Then the climate warmed, the ice sheets melted in many places, and the oceans rose. But the warming didn't last more than a few hundred thousand years. Bitter cold returned with

new sheets of thick ice. At least four times during the great Ice Age the climate changed from cold to warm to cold again. The last change back to warm melted most of the ice by about 10,000 years ago. Today ice sheets cover less than 10 percent of the earth's surface. Many scientists fear that the warming will not last and that one day in the distant future farms, villages, and great cities will be buried deep in ice.

Hidden in every inch of the earth's surface is the story of our planet. Just think about where you live. What was there a thousand years ago? A million? A billion? Was it ever underwater or under ice? Did

QUATERNARY   PRESENT

dinosaurs live there? Did the first humans hunt there? No one knows all the answers because so many changes have taken place over such a long time. Even so, by knowing how the earth works it is possible to understand how the world we live on came to look the way it does.

The powerful forces that shaped the earth's surface over the last 4.6 billion years are still shaping it today. On days when all is quiet, we hardly notice these forces at work. But on days when earthquakes destroy whole cities or lava gushes from exploding volcanoes we are stunned by how mighty these forces really are.

The first part of the Quaternary period was the time of the great Ice Age. At the edge of massive ice sheets lived large, furry mammals, such as the now extinct giant sloth and woolly mammoth. Harsh conditions forced many animals to move to warmer regions. About 10,000 years ago the Ice Age ended and the second part of the Quaternary began. It is still going on. Some of the animals shown are (a) woolly rhinoceros, (b) northern ground sloth, (c) dire wolf, (d) muskox, (e) *Panthera atrox*, (f) woolly mammoth, (g) horse, (h) large-horned bison, (i) short-faced bear.

19

crater lake

lava

hardened ash

hardened lava

vent

magma

When lava cools very quickly, it may form glassy obsidian. Indians made arrowheads out of this rock.

Tuff forms from volcanic ash. It may be welded together by the heat of an eruption.

Pumice forms from lava with gas bubbles trapped inside. It is very light and may even float on water.

A lot of yellow rhyolite can be found in Yellowstone National Park. It forms when lava cools quickly.

Dark basalt is the most common kind of igneous rock. Some islands, such as Iceland, are mostly basalt.

gas and ash cloud

Volcanoes

ONE DAY IN 1943 a Mexican farmer was working in his cornfield. He heard a loud, rumbling noise, felt the ground shake, and to his astonishment saw a large crack appear in the earth. As smoke and hot gas spewed furiously out of the crack, the terrified farmer ran to warn everyone in his village.

That night red-hot, glowing rocks and hot, powdery ash shot out of the ground like fireworks. They landed in a pile around the crack, building up into a cone that grew and grew. By the next afternoon the cone was over 120 feet (36 meters) high—and a volcano had been born.

For weeks hot rocks, ash, and gases kept shooting out of the growing volcano. Layers of ash covered the homes and fields nearby. One day hot lava started pouring out of the volcano, named Paricutin. The lava destroyed everything in its path and buried the farmer's village a mile away. By the end of the year, Paricutin was almost 1,000 ft (300 m) high—just higher than the Eiffel Tower in Paris. A river of lava had flowed out of the volcano, burying a town 5 mi (8 km) away. Only the church bell towers stood unharmed above the lava that hardened into rock.

Paricutin has not erupted since 1952. Its dramatic birth gave scientists the rare chance to witness the spectacular growth of a volcano from beginning to end. It also made a lot of people stop and wonder whether they might wake up one day and find a volcano growing in their backyard.

Magma

A volcano is an opening in the earth's crust that often forms where the crust is thin, weak, or cracked. When a volcano erupts, molten magma can escape from inside the earth. Magma is made up of liquid rock and gases that rise up toward the earth's surface from the mantle.

As magma rises, the gases in it separate from the molten rock. Sometimes they separate gently, but when magma is too thick, the gases can build up. They are very, very hot, under high pressure, and can explode violently.

Lava is a mixture of iron, oxygen, silicon, and many other elements. As lava cools, these elements combine to form mineral crystals. These crystals harden into igneous rocks. Five igneous rocks are pictured here. Others are shown on page 25.

Mount St. Helens

bulge

Sunday morning, May 18, 1980. The Cascade Range in Washington State. All is quiet around Mount St. Helens. There is a bulge on the north side of the mountain.

rock slide

Suddenly the earth shakes. Huge rocks slide down the north side of the mountain. There is a tremendous explosion at the bulge. Trees fall over for miles.

ash and gas cloud

In seconds a black cloud covers the mountain. It contains very hot gases and ash. Part of the cloud starts to move north toward the forest.

When a volcano erupts, the separated gases escape into the air, and what is left pours out as liquid rock, called lava.

Lava

Lava comes out of volcanoes in different ways. Sometimes it flies hundreds of feet in the air when a volcano "blows its top" in a great explosion. Sometimes it shoots up like a fountain of fire. Sometimes it oozes out the top or sides of an erupting volcano.

At the earth's surface lava cools rapidly and forms igneous rocks, such as basalt and pumice. The word *igneous* comes from Latin and means "formed by fire." Basalt is the most common igneous rock. If you are in Hawaii, you are standing on basalt. Basaltic rocks make up much of the sea floor, too.

When a volcano erupts, tiny lava droplets shot into the air form volcanic dust. Larger droplets form powdery ash and cinders. Little stones and large, glowing blocks can also be thrown out with lava sprayed into the air.

Most of the time lava, cinders, and ash pile up around a volcano's opening, or vent. They build up into heaps called cones that can grow into mountains, like Paricutin. At the top of many volcanic mountains there is a funnel-shaped crater. Sometimes the top of a volcano collapses, fills with rain and melted snow, and becomes a lake.

A Volcano Awakes with Fury

At 8:30 A.M. that Sunday morning in 1980, many people in Washington State were eating breakfast. Others were reading or driving their cars. Not one of them had any idea that within two minutes, Mount St. Helens would wake from its 123-year sleep and make headlines around the world by erupting violently.

For weeks scientists had warned that Mount St. Helens might erupt soon. It had been the scene of minor earthquakes. That very morning, two geologists were flying over the mountain to inspect it. From directly overhead they saw the mountain begin to shake and huge rocks slide down the north slope. Suddenly the north slope exploded with more power than hundreds of atomic bombs. A giant cloud of steam, hot gases, and ash rose up and the plane dived, barely avoiding being destroyed.

By the time the plane landed the cloud had swept down the mountain, moved north through a forest, and killed nearly every living thing in its way.

Millions of tons of hot ash were blasted high in the sky, then carried for days by strong winds to cities and towns hundreds of miles away. In some places the air was so thick with ash that noon seemed as dark as midnight.

The eruption of Mount St. Helens flattened trees for miles. Heat from the volcano quickly melted ice and snow, causing thick mud to form. The hot mud raced down the mountain slope, carrying trees, ash, and rocks into the nearby river valley. More than 50 people were killed, and the explosion lowered the volcano by more than 1,200 ft (360 m).

Mount St. Helens stayed active for months, then fell back to sleep. Geologists continue to study it as they try to find a way to predict when volcanoes will erupt.

new crater

lava and mud

When the cloud clears, all is in ruins. The forest is destroyed, and animals lie dead. Lava and thick mud flow down the mountain. Mount St. Helens is over 1,200 ft (360 m) lower and has a large, new crater.

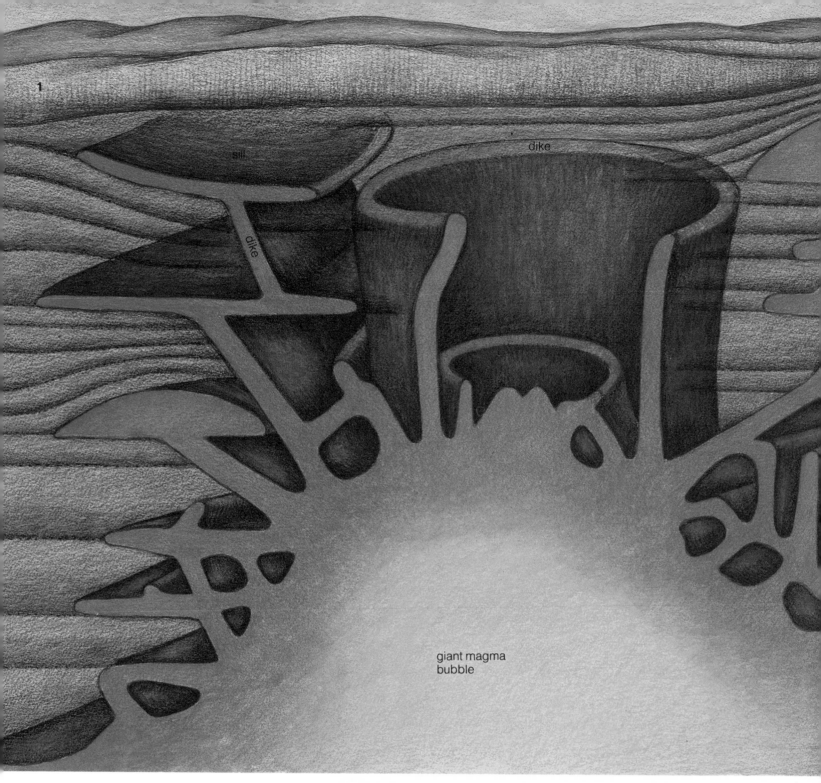

1

sill

dike

dike

dike

giant magma
bubble

(**1**) A giant bubble of hot magma collects in the earth's crust. Some of the magma forces its way between layers of other rocks, forming sills, dikes, and laccoliths. (**2**) After thousands or millions of years the magma cools and forms igneous rocks. (**3**) When the rocks above wear away, the upper parts of a sill, dike, and laccolith are on the earth's surface. The larger, deeper batholith is still hidden.

24

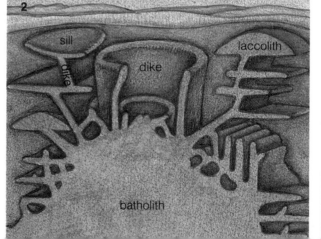

3

sill

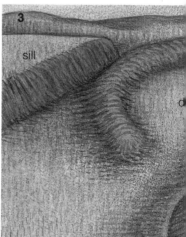

2

sill

dike

dike

laccolith

batholith

gabbro

diabase

diorite

peridotite

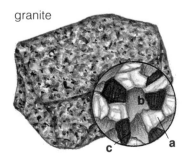
granite

laccolith

Rocks from Magma

INSIDE THE EARTH'S CRUST there are igneous rocks that didn't form from lava. Why are they called igneous rocks? Because, like lava rocks, they were "formed by fire"—fiery magma.

Countless times in the earth's history hot magma has risen up toward the earth's surface without reaching it. Instead the magma collected in gigantic bubbles inside the crust. Very slowly, the minerals in the magma bubbles cooled and hardened. They formed igneous rocks, such as gabbro and granite. Granite is the very hard rock that is used in monuments and buildings. Granitic rocks are also the main type of rock that makes up the continents we live on.

Lith *Means Stone*

Geologists call the largest magma bubbles that solidify below the earth's surface batholiths. The word *batholith* means "deep stone." Some batholiths are hundreds of miles long, over 60 mi (96 km) wide, and perhaps 19 mi (30 km) deep.

The illustrations show that not all of the magma stays in the bubbles. Some can spread out between rock layers around it, forming sills. Some can cut up and down through rock layers, forming dikes. And some can squeeze up into smaller bubbles, called laccoliths ("lakes of stone"). Laccoliths near the surface push on the rocks above and arch them up to form domes.

In many parts of the world, igneous rocks remain hidden by thick layers of other rocks above them. In many places, though, those other rocks have been completely worn away, exposing the tops of batholiths in Idaho and California, dikes in New Mexico, and laccoliths in South Dakota and Utah. And the Palisades cliffs along the Hudson River in New York State are really a sill hundreds of feet thick.

Magma that cools inside the earth's crust forms different kinds of igneous rocks. Gabbro, diabase, peridotite, and granite are shown here. Some granites are made of the minerals quartz (a), feldspar (b), and mica (c).

25

Weathering

From mountaintops to deserts, rocks are under attack. They are being broken into smaller and smaller pieces by the process called weathering.

Weathering is a powerful force that continually changes the land. It destroys mountains, creates deep grooves in cliffs, and peels giant slabs of rock off hills. In one way or another, it has helped shape nearly every rock you have ever seen.

Most of the time, weathering takes place so slowly and quietly that hardly anyone notices it. But go to a park and you can find signs of it all around. Pick up some small rocks—they were broken off larger rocks by weathering. Pull a loose chip off a big rock—it was loosened by weathering. The rock that crumbles in your hand was weakened by weathering. The tree growing out of a crack in a rock is breaking that rock open. The sand and most of the soil were formed by weathering.

Weathering doesn't just attack rocks. The rusty nails and peeling paint you see on park benches were caused by weathering. So were cracks in the sidewalk and potholes in the street.

Agents of Weathering

Weathering is produced by agents such as water, ice, and gases in the atmosphere. These agents work in two basic ways. In mechanical weathering, they break larger rocks into smaller rocks without changing the minerals in them. In chemical weathering they change the minerals in rocks, causing the rocks to weaken and eventually crumble. Either way, the agents of weathering break rocks into pieces (but do not carry them away like the forces of erosion do; see page 56).

Mechanical Weathering

Mechanical weathering takes place in a number of ways. One, called frost action, involves water and ice.

Water seeps into cracks and holes in rocks. In places where the temperature falls below freezing, this water turns into ice. When water changes from a liquid into a solid, it expands and takes up more space. It pushes out with a force strong enough to open the crack even farther. When the ice melts, more water can seep into

(Above) It is the Cretaceous period, 100 million years ago. A brontosaurus feeds on plants. Beneath the ground hot magma has cooled to form a sill, dike, and laccolith. (Below) It is the Quaternary period, 1 million years ago. The rocks above the sill and the dike have been slowly broken up by weathering and carried away by erosion (page 56). A woolly mammoth walks above the laccolith, which is still completely hidden underground. The mammoth can see the edge of the sill and the top of the dike. (Right) Today the upper parts of the sill, dike, and laccolith are all exposed to the agents of weathering and erosion. Because the sill, dike, and laccolith are made of very hard igneous rocks, they weather more slowly than most of the other rocks around them.

26

Ice, plants, air, and water attack cliff rocks and cause bits and pieces to break off the top and face of the cliff. These pieces tumble to the foot of the cliff and pile up into a talus slope. (*Talus* is Latin for "ankle.") Both the cliff rocks and the fallen rocks continue to weather mechanically and chemically.

the enlarged crack. If this water freezes too, the crack will grow even larger. Over time, the growing crack will split the rock apart.

Plants also split rocks apart by mechanical weathering. Their roots reach into the cracks in rocks, grow, and push against the rocks. The force of the pushing enlarges old cracks and even forms new ones.

Chemical Weathering

Chemical weathering changes minerals in rocks. The changed minerals weaken the structure of rocks so much that the rocks crumble. This is what happens when oxygen in the air attacks rocks that contain minerals with iron in them. The oxygen combines with the iron and turns it into a powdery rust.

Rainwater causes chemical weathering too. As rain falls, it combines with some of the carbon dioxide gas that is in the air and becomes a weak acid, like soda water. This acid changes many minerals and even dissolves some away. Over time the changed minerals fall apart and the rocks they are in break into pieces.

Both chemical and mechanical weathering take place very slowly. Even so, some rocks weather more rapidly than others. Strange as it may sound, one of the best places to see examples of this is in a cemetery that has old tombstones. As you walk along, you may see a tombstone from 1750 with letters you can clearly read. Close by, there may be a stone from 1850, made of different rock, with letters nearly worn away by weathering. In general, soft rocks, cracked rocks, rocks made of minerals that easily dissolve, and rocks in moist climates weather more quickly than other rocks do.

Soil

The soil we depend on for so much of our food is a mixture of bits and pieces of weathered rock. It contains minerals, water, air, and decayed parts of plants and animals. Soil usually forms in three layers, which are shown on pages 30 and 31.

Most plants live in soil. So do earthworms, ants, moles, and many other animals. As these animals dig and tunnel along, they loosen soil and mix it. They push rock chips up to the surface, where most weathering takes place. And they make spaces that let air and water reach rocks under soil and weather them, too.

talus slope

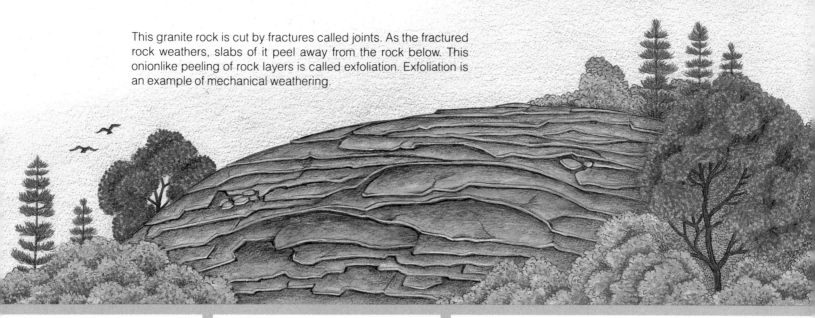

This granite rock is cut by fractures called joints. As the fractured rock weathers, slabs of it peel away from the rock below. This onionlike peeling of rock layers is called exfoliation. Exfoliation is an example of mechanical weathering.

rust

Basalt contains minerals with iron in them. Oxygen in the air combines with iron to form rust, or iron oxide. Iron oxide colors some rocks and soils red or brown.

The name and dates on this tombstone have been dissolved away by chemical weathering.

These plants are growing in soil trapped in rock cracks. In their search for minerals and water, the roots push on the rocks and make the cracks larger. Growing roots often force rocks to split apart.

The edges and corners of rocks are gradually rounded as the rocks weather.

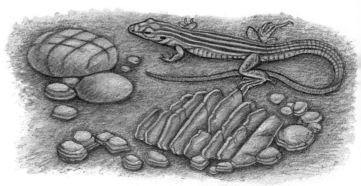

In many deserts it is hot and dry during the day and very cool at night. Such daily heating and cooling makes rocks expand and contract, which helps break apart rocks weakened by weathering.

Soil

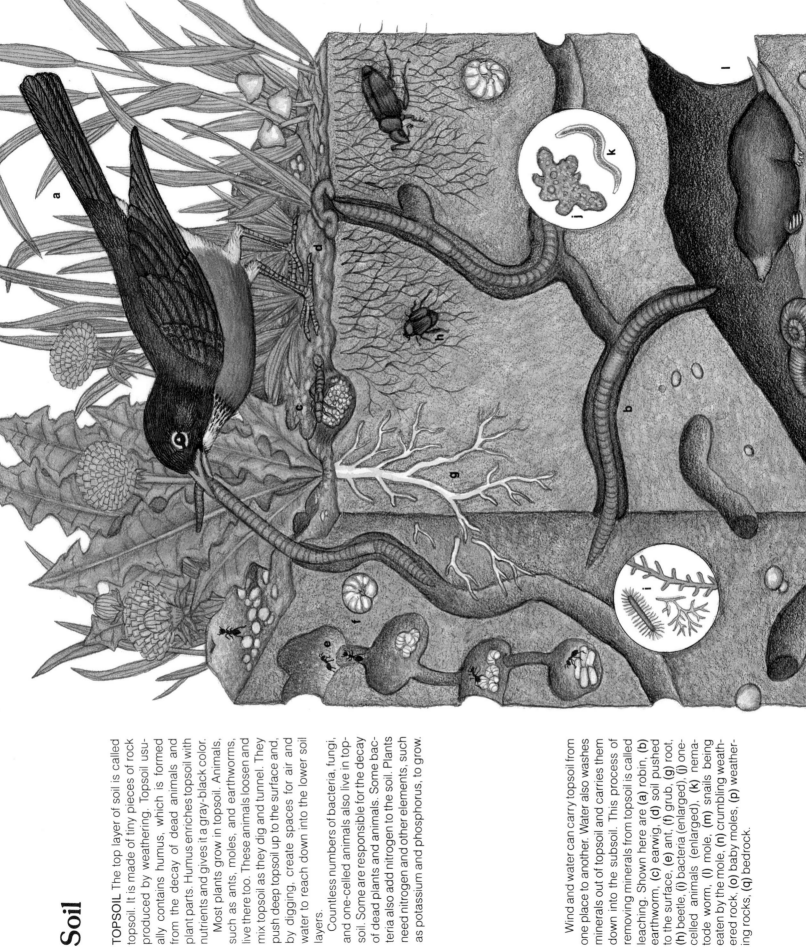

TOPSOIL The top layer of soil is called topsoil. It is made of tiny pieces of rock produced by weathering. Topsoil usually contains humus, which is formed from the decay of dead animals and plant parts. Humus enriches topsoil with nutrients and gives it a gray-black color.

Most plants grow in topsoil. Animals, such as ants, moles, and earthworms, live there too. These animals loosen and mix topsoil as they dig and tunnel. They push deep topsoil up to the surface and, by digging, create spaces for air and water to reach down into the lower soil layers.

Countless numbers of bacteria, fungi, and one-celled animals also live in topsoil. Some are responsible for the decay of dead plants and animals. Some bacteria also add nitrogen to the soil. Plants need nitrogen and other elements, such as potassium and phosphorus, to grow.

Wind and water can carry topsoil from one place to another. Water also washes minerals out of topsoil and carries them down into the subsoil. This process of removing minerals from topsoil is called leaching. Shown here are **(a)** robin, **(b)** earthworm, **(c)** earwig, **(d)** soil pushed to the surface, **(e)** ant, **(f)** grub, **(g)** root, **(h)** beetle, **(i)** bacteria (enlarged), **(j)** one-celled animals (enlarged), **(k)** nematode worm, **(l)** mole, **(m)** snails being eaten by the mole, **(n)** crumbling weathered rock, **(o)** baby moles, **(p)** weathering rocks, **(q)** bedrock.

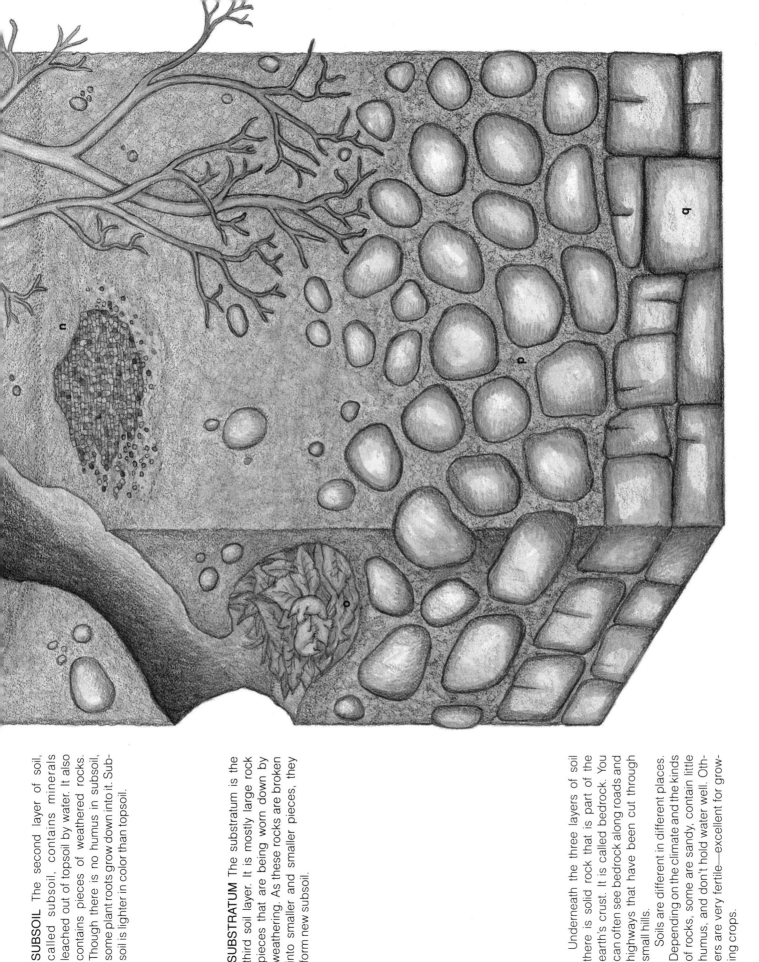

SUBSOIL The second layer of soil, called subsoil, contains minerals leached out of topsoil by water. It also contains pieces of weathered rocks. Though there is no humus in subsoil, some plant roots grow down into it. Subsoil is lighter in color than topsoil.

SUBSTRATUM The substratum is the third soil layer. It is mostly large rock pieces that are being worn down by weathering. As these rocks are broken into smaller and smaller pieces, they form new subsoil.

Underneath the three layers of soil there is solid rock that is part of the earth's crust. It is called bedrock. You can often see bedrock along roads and highways that have been cut through small hills.

Soils are different in different places. Depending on the climate and the kinds of rocks, some are sandy, contain little humus, and don't hold water well. Others are very fertile—excellent for growing crops.

Layered Rock

IN NORTHERN ARIZONA you can visit the greatest river canyon in the world—the Grand Canyon. By foot or on a mule you can journey for hours to the bottom of this mile-deep natural wonder. Along the way down you will pass thick and thin layers of colorful rocks: gray sandstone, pink limestone, red shale, brown sandstone, white limestone. None of these rock layers was formed from lava or magma. The layers are not made of igneous rocks, but of sedimentary rocks.

The word *sedimentary* comes from Latin and means "settling." Sedimentary rocks form from sediment that settles in layers. Mud in a river is sediment. So are pebbles in a stream and sand on the beach. In fact, all kinds of weathered rocks are sediment, and geologists have grouped them together by size. The largest are called boulders and cobbles (see the illustration on page 33). Then comes pebbles and granules, followed by sand, silt, and clay. When clay and silt become wet, they form mud.

(a) Tons of loose, weathered rocks sometimes pile up on mountain slopes. After heavy rains these rocks can suddenly slide down in an avalanche. At the bottom they break up even more as one rock smashes into another. (b) Heavy boulders and cobbles remain where they fall in the river. (c) Fast-moving river waters carry pebbles, silt, sand, and clay toward the ocean. (d) A stream delivers more rocks into the river. (e) Strong winds blow sand into the river and the sea. (f) Rivers deliver millions of tons of weathered rocks into the ocean.

Most sedimentary rocks form at the bottom of the oceans. Some form at the bottom of lakes, swamps, and streams. How sediment winds up underwater and then becomes pressed into sedimentary rocks is really the story of how new rocks are made from pieces of older ones.

Delivering Sediments

Whether you live in the city, or the country, or near the seashore, you have probably watched heavy rains wash away soil, sand, pebbles, and other weathered rocks. Rain washes these sediments into streams, and streams carry them into lakes and rivers.

Most rivers flow into the sea. Night and day, year after year, they deliver tons of sediment from the land into ocean waters. When a river enters the ocean, it slows down and deposits pebbles and granules mostly near shore. The lighter sand is picked up by ocean currents and carried away from shore, where it begins to settle to the bottom. The even lighter silt and clay are carried into deeper waters, where they too eventually settle to the sea floor.

Weathered rocks are one kind of sediment. They are divided into different groups by size. The largest are called boulders, the smallest are silt and clay.

pebbles

granules

cobble

sand

silt

boulder

glacier

a

d

b

c

g

h

Sedimentary rocks can form in many places: **(a)** siltstone, at the bottom of a lake; **(b)** chalk, in shallow sea waters; **(c)** coral limestone, on a coral reef; **(d)** mudstone, near a river that often floods; **(e)** rock salt and gypsum, in a desert that was once underwater; **(f)** sandstone, near shore; **(g)** limestone, farther out at sea; **(h)** shale, away from shore.

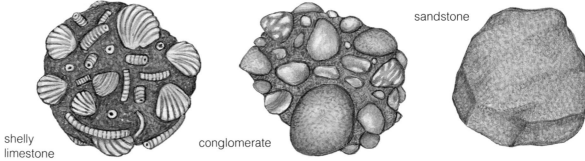

These are some sedimentary rocks. Conglomerate forms from rounded pebbles that are cemented together. Sandstone has small openings, or pores, among its cemented sand grains. Shale forms from silt and clay. It splits into layers and crumbles easily.

shelly limestone

conglomerate

sandstone

talus slope

e

f

sandstone
layers

From Sediment to Rock

Wherever sediment sinks in lakes or in the sea, it settles in layers on top of other sediment. Each new layer presses down on the layers beneath it. As the upper layers thicken, they squeeze out water and press the lower layers together. With silt and clay the pressure of the upper layers can become so intense that the lower layers actually stick together. Over a long time the lower layers are pressed into sedimentary rocks such as shale and mudstone.

Because sand, granules, and pebbles are larger and harder than silt and clay, they aren't pressed together as tightly by the layers of sediment above them. The spaces that remain become filled with minerals from the water. These minerals act like cement. They cement sand into sandstone, and granules and pebbles into a rock called conglomerate.

Other Sediments

Many tiny sea plants (algae) and animals have shells. When these animals and plants die, their shells settle to the sea floor as sediment. Combined with bones and teeth from other dead animals, this sediment builds up in layers. Over time these layers become pressed and cemented together, forming limestones such as coquina and natural chalk.

Another kind of sediment comes from minerals that were once dissolved in water. When the water evaporates, the minerals are left behind as layers of sediment that form rocks, such as rock salt and gypsum.

If you were to walk across this continent, about 75 percent of the rocks you would see are sedimentary. Throughout the earth's history most parts of the land were covered by seawater. During those times layers of sediment were deposited that formed sedimentary rocks. When the seas retreated, these rocks became part of the land. Often the same land was flooded again and again, for long periods of time. New layers of sedimentary rocks formed on top of older layers. You can see this in the Grand Canyon, where the deeper you go, the older and older the rocks become.

At the bottom of the Grand Canyon is the Colorado River. Right now its rushing brown waters are carrying away sediment produced by the weathering of the canyon walls. This same sediment may eventually form a rock somewhere else.

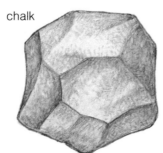

chalk

shale

Fossils

Scientists who study fossils are called paleontologists. They often find fossils in layers of sandstone, limestone, and shale. The oldest fossils in this cliff are in the lowest rock layers. More recent fossils are in the layers above. Fish fossils found on land are clues that the land was once underwater. **(a)** Imprint of a giant winged insect from the Carboniferous period. **(b)** Fish skeleton from the Permian period. **(c)** Dinosaur bone from the Cretaceous period.

No one has ever seen a stegosaurus, a brontosaurus, or any other dinosaur. As everyone knows, the last of the dinosaurs died out millions of years ago. Even so, we know a lot about dinosaurs from studying their fossils. Fossils are anything left of plants, animals, and people that lived a very long time ago.

When most ancient plants and animals died, they either decayed completely or were eaten. Some, though, were buried quickly by mud when they fell into swamps, lakes, and shallow ocean waters. These buried plant and animal bodies slowly rotted away. Sometimes hard bones, teeth, and shells remained and were pressed under layers of sediment. In time the sediment layers formed sedimentary rocks with the plant and animal remains trapped inside as fossils.

Kinds of Fossils

There are several kinds of fossils. Some are unchanged bones, teeth, and shells of dead animals. Others (page 37) are plant and animal parts that have been changed—wood that has turned into stone, bones that have filled with hardened minerals, leaf outlines that have been pressed into rock, and footprints that have been left in hardened mud.

Fossils have been found in places other than rock. The bones of saber-toothed tigers were found in tar pits in Los Angeles. Insects, millions of years old, have been found in hardened tree sap, called amber. And an entire woolly mammoth was discovered in Siberia in a huge chunk of glacial ice.

Fossils help scientists piece together the story of the earth. They reveal which kinds of plants and animals lived during different periods of the earth's history. They show that many species of plants and animals that once lived on the earth no longer exist. Fossils, however, do not reveal the complete story of life on the earth. Scientists suspect, but cannot yet prove, that millions of species of plants and animals lived and died without leaving any fossils behind. Perhaps you will be lucky enough to find a fossil of a creature that nobody has yet discovered.

(1) When this lampshell died, it was quickly buried by layers of sand. The soft lampshell animal in the shell rotted away.

(2) Over time the sand became cemented into sandstone.

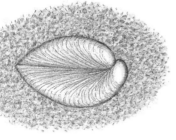

(3) Water seeped inside the sandstone and dissolved away the shell. An empty cavity, or mold, in the shape of the shell was left in the rock.

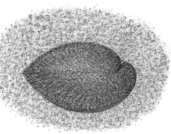

(4) Minerals from the water slowly filled the mold. They hardened into a stone copy, or cast, of the shell shape. Both the mold and the cast are fossils.

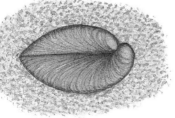

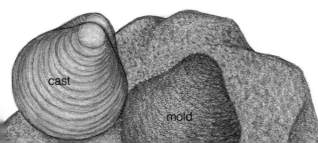

cast

mold

FOSSILS (a) Some dead trees were buried quickly and groundwater seeped through them. Little by little, minerals in the water replaced all of the wood. The minerals hardened, causing the trees to petrify, or turn to stone. Some fossil bones are also petrified. **(b)** A buried leaf was pressed between sediment layers that became sedimentary rock. The leaf disappeared but left its fossil imprint in the rock. **(c)** An unchanged tooth from a shark that lived about 20 million years ago. **(d)** Millions of years ago this insect was trapped in tree sap. The sap hardened into transparent amber with the insect fossil preserved inside. **(e)** A dinosaur made these footprints in soft mud. The mud hardened and eventually turned into rock.

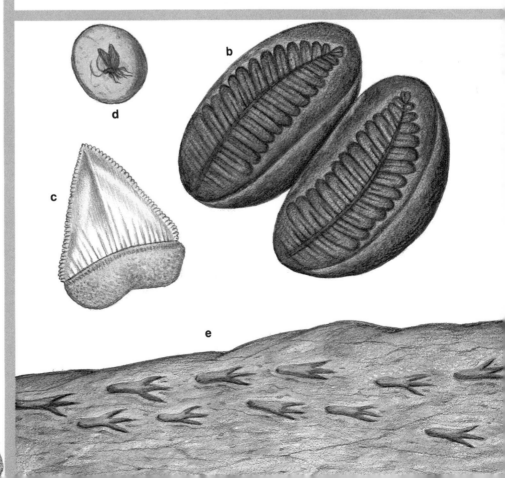

b

d

c

e

All coal was once peat. Peat formed millions of years ago from layers of plants that fell into swamps and were buried under sediments. Like all other plants, these plants had absorbed light energy from the sun and stored it as chemical energy. This energy was retained as the peat became lignite coal and the lignite became bituminous coal. When coal is burned today, it gives off energy from sunlight stored for millions of years!

lignite

bituminous

anthracite

peat

lignite

bituminous

anthracite

Both lignite and bituminous coal are sedimentary rocks. Most of the coal we use is bituminous. Anthracite coal is a metamorphic rock (page 45). When it is burned, it gives off a lot less smoke than bituminous.

peat

The Story of Coal

COAL IS one of the most important rocks found on the earth. It looks and feels like other rocks, but instead of being made of minerals, it is mostly carbon from ancient plants. When it is burned, it gives off enough energy to heat homes and generate electricity. Coal took millions of years to form, and once we burn all of it, we have no way of making any more.

How Coal Formed

Most of the coal we use today formed from plants that lived between 250 and 400 million years ago in large, swampy forests. Often when these plants died, they fell into the swamps and began to rot. The rotting process, however, stopped before it was completed because of a lack of oxygen in the swamp waters. Thick layers of partially rotted plants collected and, in time, formed a soft, brown material called peat.

Later the swamps became lakes or were flooded by rivers or seawater. Layers of sand, silt, and clay deposited on top of the peat pressed down and squeezed much of the water out of it. This pressing also heated the peat. As a result of both the heat and the pressure, the peat hardened into the sedimentary rock called brown coal, or lignite.

As more layers of sediment were deposited on top of the lignite, the pressure and heat increased. The brown lignite became the soft, black coal called bituminous. Bituminous is also a sedimentary rock. In places new mountains were raised on land where the bituminous had formed. The intense heat and pressure of mountain building (page 80) changed some of the bituminous into anthracite, a very hard, black coal.

Fuel from Fossils

If you look at a piece of coal under a magnifying glass, you can sometimes see parts of leaves, bark, and wood in it. Because it formed from the remains of ancient plants, coal is called a fossil fuel.

As a fuel, coal supplies about one fifth of our energy

39

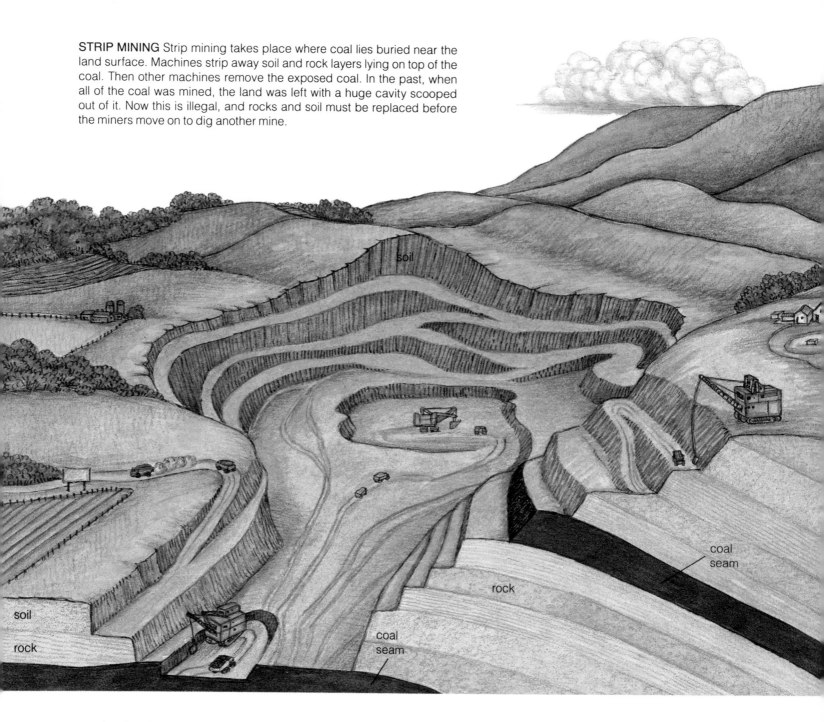

STRIP MINING Strip mining takes place where coal lies buried near the land surface. Machines strip away soil and rock layers lying on top of the coal. Then other machines remove the exposed coal. In the past, when all of the coal was mined, the land was left with a huge cavity scooped out of it. Now this is illegal, and rocks and soil must be replaced before the miners move on to dig another mine.

soil

coal
seam

rock

soil

rock

coal
seam

needs. It also provides raw materials used to make plastics, perfumes, and some medicines. Many geologists think that at the rate we are using it today, the world's supply of coal will last about 250 more years.

Mining Coal

Coal is found underground in layers called seams. Some seams are close to the surface; most others are buried deep under layers of sedimentary rocks. The coal in a seam has to be mined in order for people to use it. Some of the different ways of mining coal are illustrated on these pages.

Coal mining can be costly and dangerous. It can destroy parts of the land. Coal itself also creates problems as a fuel. When it is burned, it gives off ash and gases that can pollute the air. These gases can combine with rain and turn it acidic. Acid rain may harm animals and plants, and even damage buildings. People are trying to find ways to mine and burn coal without causing any harm.

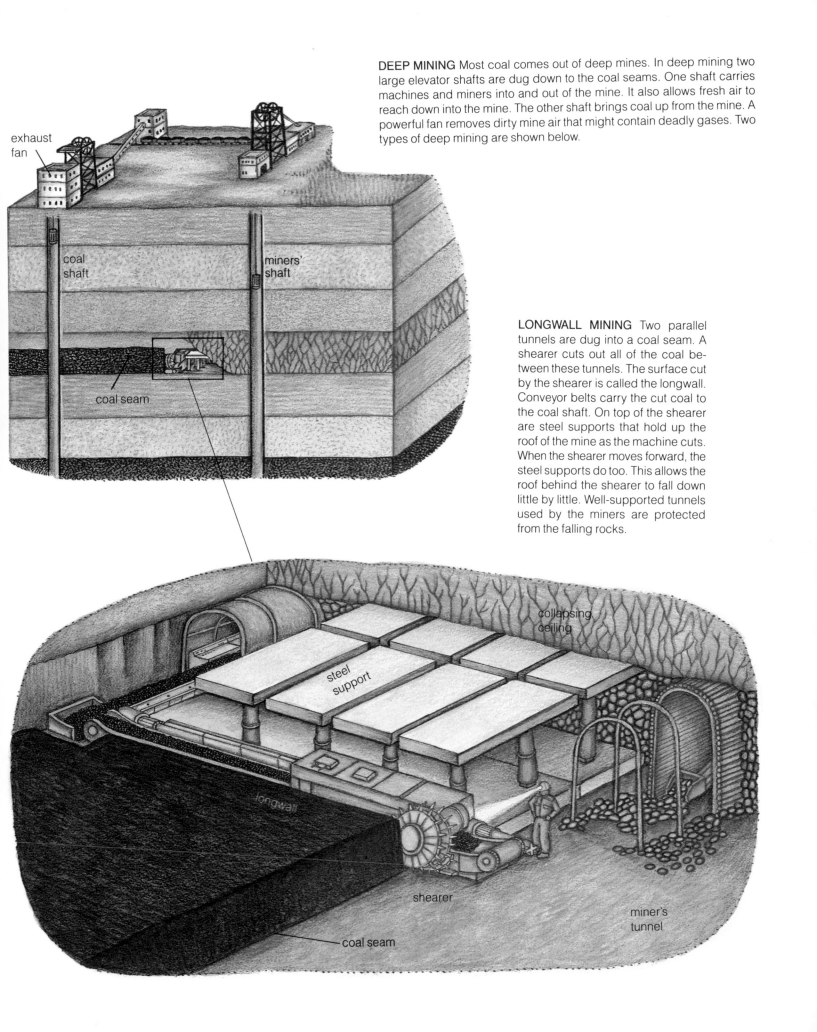

DEEP MINING Most coal comes out of deep mines. In deep mining two large elevator shafts are dug down to the coal seams. One shaft carries machines and miners into and out of the mine. It also allows fresh air to reach down into the mine. The other shaft brings coal up from the mine. A powerful fan removes dirty mine air that might contain deadly gases. Two types of deep mining are shown below.

exhaust fan

coal shaft

miners' shaft

coal seam

LONGWALL MINING Two parallel tunnels are dug into a coal seam. A shearer cuts out all of the coal between these tunnels. The surface cut by the shearer is called the longwall. Conveyor belts carry the cut coal to the coal shaft. On top of the shearer are steel supports that hold up the roof of the mine as the machine cuts. When the shearer moves forward, the steel supports do too. This allows the roof behind the shearer to fall down little by little. Well-supported tunnels used by the miners are protected from the falling rocks.

collapsing ceiling

steel support

longwall

shearer

miner's tunnel

coal seam

Petroleum and Natural Gas

Every hour of every day, millions of gallons of gasoline, kerosene, fuel oil, and diesel oil are burned all over the world. These liquid fuels are produced from petroleum, a resource so vital to our modern way of life that nations go to war over it.

Petroleum and natural gas formed over millions of years from the decaying bodies of sea plants and animals. These bodies were buried and pressed under layers of sediment, then baked by heat deep in the earth's crust. This baking and pressing produced petro-leum and gas, which soaked into the small openings in neighboring rocks, such as sandstone. But when the petroleum and gas reached rock they could not pass through, such as shale, they became trapped. Only by drilling wells through the shale can we bring these trapped resources to the surface.

Today petroleum and natural gas provide over 66 percent of our energy needs. But we are burning these fossil fuels up so fast that many geologists fear that there will be next to none left on the earth in 100 years. Then it will take millions of years for more of these precious fossil fuels to form.

derrick

pump

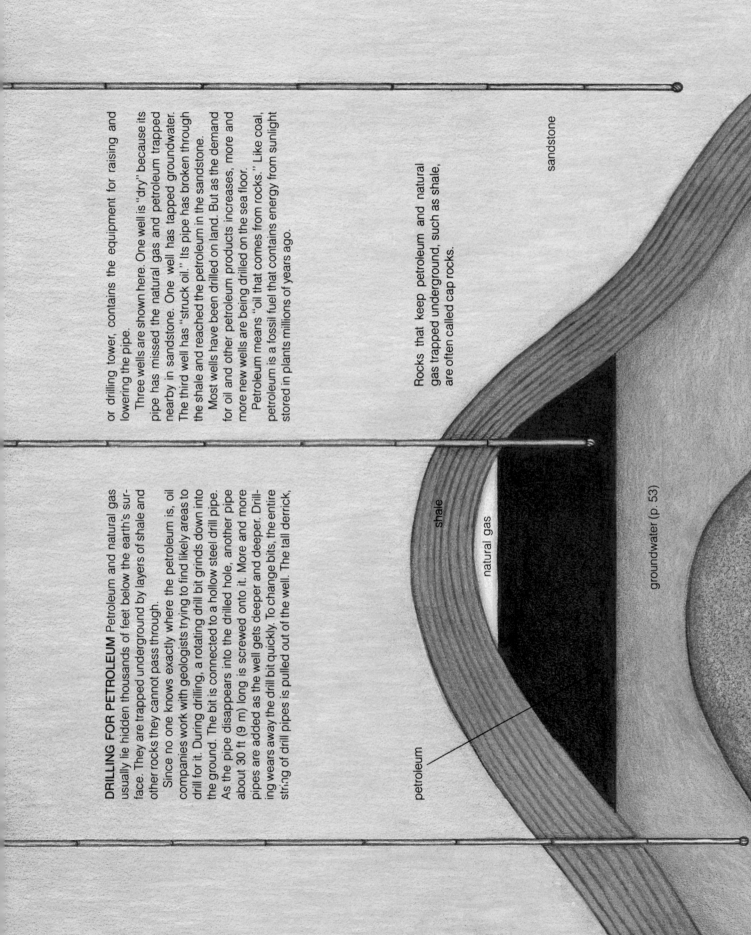

DRILLING FOR PETROLEUM Petroleum and natural gas usually lie hidden thousands of feet below the earth's surface. They are trapped underground by layers of shale and other rocks they cannot pass through.

Since no one knows exactly where the petroleum is, oil companies work with geologists trying to find likely areas to drill for it. During drilling, a rotating drill bit grinds down into the ground. The bit is connected to a hollow steel drill pipe. As the pipe disappears into the drilled hole, another pipe about 30 ft (9 m) long is screwed onto it. More and more pipes are added as the well gets deeper and deeper. Drilling wears away the drill bit quickly. To change bits, the entire string of drill pipes is pulled out of the well. The tall derrick,

or drilling tower, contains the equipment for raising and lowering the pipe.

Three wells are shown here. One well is "dry" because its pipe has missed the natural gas and petroleum trapped nearby in sandstone. One well has tapped groundwater. The third well has "struck oil." Its pipe has broken through the shale and reached the petroleum in the sandstone.

Most wells have been drilled on land. But as the demand for oil and other petroleum products increases, more and more new wells are being drilled on the sea floor.

Petroleum means "oil that comes from rocks." Like coal, petroleum is a fossil fuel that contains energy from sunlight stored in plants millions of years ago.

Rocks that keep petroleum and natural gas trapped underground, such as shale, are often called cap rocks.

sandstone

shale

natural gas

petroleum

groundwater (p. 53)

METAMORPHIC ROCKS Slate forms from shale. Because it is very hard and splits into flat sheets, it is often used to make flooring, roof tiles, and chalkboards. Mica schist can also form from shale. Like slate, it splits into thin layers. Granite gneiss forms from granite, and quartzite from sandstone. Intense heat or pressure can change limestone into marble. Pure marble is white, but marble can be colored black, green, yellow, or pink by minerals it contains.

slate

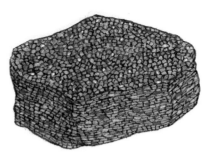

mica schist

granite gneiss

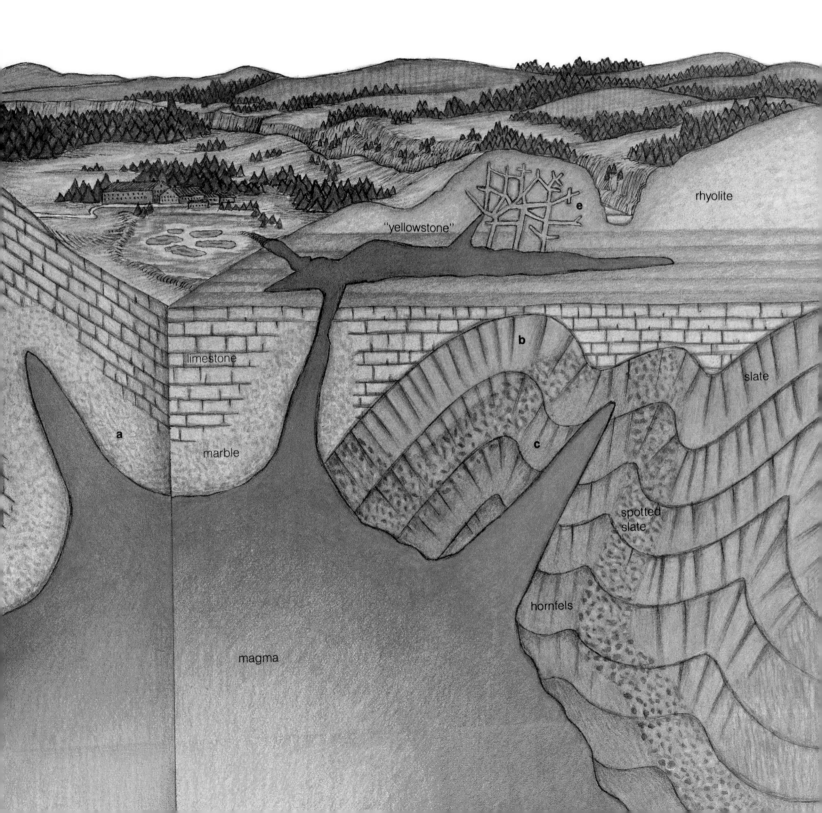

rhyolite

"yellowstone"

e

limestone

a

marble

magma

b

c

slate

spotted slate

hornfels

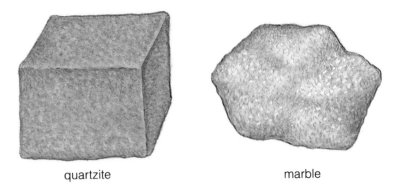

quartzite   marble

Changed Rocks

Take popping corn, heat it high enough, and you get popcorn. Take a soda can, squeeze it hard enough, and you can get a flat piece of metal. Take an igneous or a sedimentary rock, heat or press it just enough, and yes—it changes too. It changes into a new kind of rock, called a metamorphic rock. *Metamorphic* means "changed form."

Of course, no person can heat or press a rock enough to make it change form, but inside the earth's crust intense heat and pressure are changing rocks. They are changing limestone into marble, shale into slate, and sandstone into quartzite. Marble, slate, and quartzite are all metamorphic rocks.

Any igneous or sedimentary rock can be changed into a metamorphic rock. Even a metamorphic rock can be changed for a second time into another metamorphic rock. Some of the ways in which metamorphic rocks are formed are illustrated on these pages.

The Rock Cycle

Over and over again, new rocks form in the world we live on. Igneous rocks harden from lava and magma. Sedimentary rocks form from bits and pieces of other rocks. And nearly all metamorphic rocks form from igneous and sedimentary rocks.

Rocks are broken down by the agents of weathering. Some rocks are even forced down inside the earth, where they melt into new magma (page 78). This new magma can form more igneous rocks.

The never-ending process of rocks forming, being broken down, and being changed is called the rock cycle. You will find out more about how the rock cycle works on page 88.

phyllite

d

garnet schist

Here are some of the ways in which metamorphic rocks are formed: **(a)** Hot magma rose inside the earth's crust and heated limestone around it. The intense heat changed the limestone into marble. **(b)** Once there were layers of shale here. High pressure changed the shale into slate. **(c)** Slate is already a metamorphic rock. Even so, hot magma baked the slate, changing it into spotted slate and hornfels. Both are metamorphic rocks too. **(d)** In this region intense heat and pressure changed the slate into phyllite and garnet schist. **(e)** Very hot water that escaped from magma changed rhyolite into "yellowstone."

45

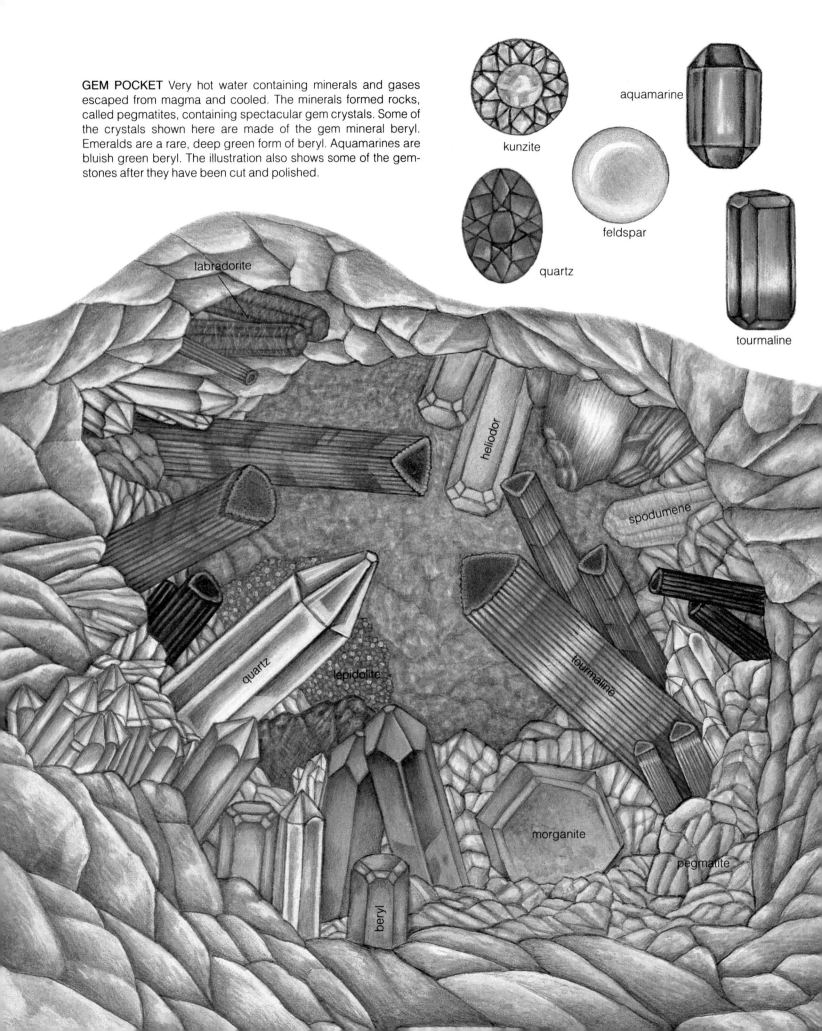

GEM POCKET Very hot water containing minerals and gases escaped from magma and cooled. The minerals formed rocks, called pegmatites, containing spectacular gem crystals. Some of the crystals shown here are made of the gem mineral beryl. Emeralds are a rare, deep green form of beryl. Aquamarines are bluish green beryl. The illustration also shows some of the gemstones after they have been cut and polished.

kunzite

aquamarine

feldspar

quartz

tourmaline

labradorite

heliodor

spodumene

quartz

lepidolite

tourmaline

morganite

beryl

pegmatite

Gemstones

Gemstones are minerals found inside certain rocks. They are prized for their beauty, size, and color. Many gemstones are very hard and difficult to scratch. The gemstone diamond is the hardest of all minerals. It is so hard that it is used to cut glass.

Emeralds, rubies, sapphires, and other gemstones can be cut and polished to create sparkling jewels. Because gemstones are so valuable, some people will do almost anything to get them.

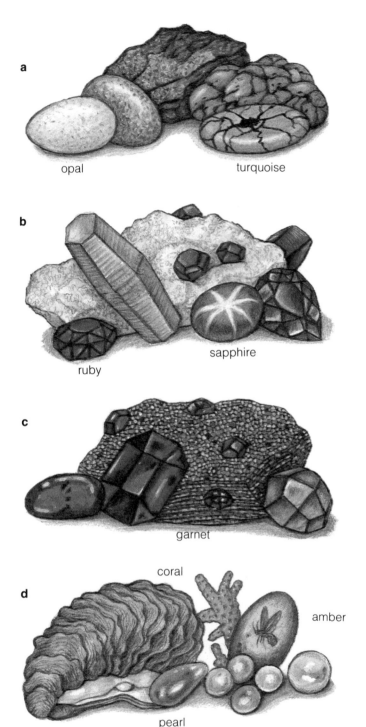

a

opal   turquoise

b

ruby   sapphire

c

garnet

d

coral   amber

pearl

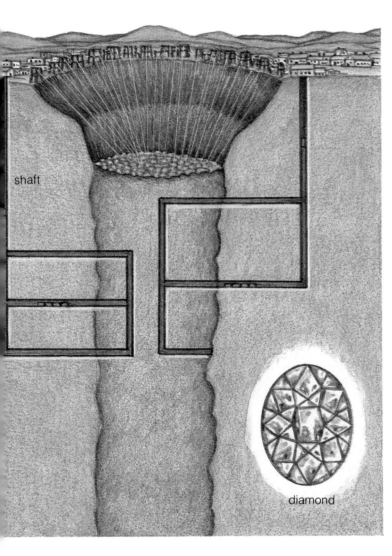

shaft

diamond

Diamonds are actually pure carbon. They form deep inside the earth's crust under extreme heat and pressure. In the diamond mine shown above, diamonds were first dug out of the open pit. Then shafts were dug to mine deep for more diamonds.

GEMSTONES (a) Opal is found in igneous and sedimentary rocks. When it reflects light, a rainbow of color can often be seen in it. Beautiful turquoise stones are used by many western Indians in their jewelry. (b) Both rubies and sapphires are types of the hard mineral corundum. Rubies, which are red corundum, are very rare and extremely valuable. When star sapphires reflect light, a six-pointed star can be seen in them. (c) Garnet is often found in mica schist rocks. (d) Amber, coral, and pearls are valued gems, but they are not gemstones. Amber is hardened tree sap, coral is made by tiny coral animals that live in warm sea waters, and pearls form inside oysters.

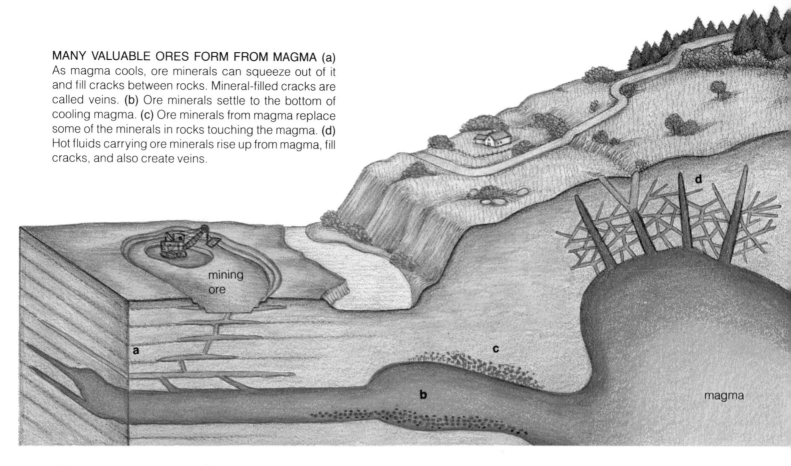

MANY VALUABLE ORES FORM FROM MAGMA (a) As magma cools, ore minerals can squeeze out of it and fill cracks between rocks. Mineral-filled cracks are called veins. **(b)** Ore minerals settle to the bottom of cooling magma. **(c)** Ore minerals from magma replace some of the minerals in rocks touching the magma. **(d)** Hot fluids carrying ore minerals rise up from magma, fill cracks, and also create veins.

mining ore

d

a

c

b

magma

Ores

Iron in steel, copper in wires, aluminum in aircraft, lead in batteries: each of these important metals comes from minerals found in rocks. When a mineral contains enough metal that the metal can be mined for a profit, the mineral is called an ore.

Most of the iron we use comes from the minerals hematite, magnetite, and ilmenite. These iron ores are often found near the earth's surface and are mined from open pits. Gold and silver are often found in pure form filling cracks, or veins, between rocks. Veins can contain so much valuable metal that it is worth digging deep to reach them.

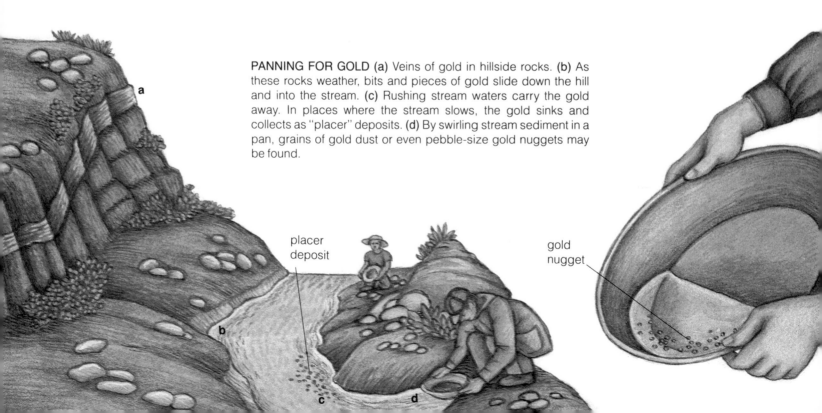

PANNING FOR GOLD (a) Veins of gold in hillside rocks. **(b)** As these rocks weather, bits and pieces of gold slide down the hill and into the stream. **(c)** Rushing stream waters carry the gold away. In places where the stream slows, the gold sinks and collects as "placer" deposits. **(d)** By swirling stream sediment in a pan, grains of gold dust or even pebble-size gold nuggets may be found.

a

placer deposit

b

c

d

gold nugget

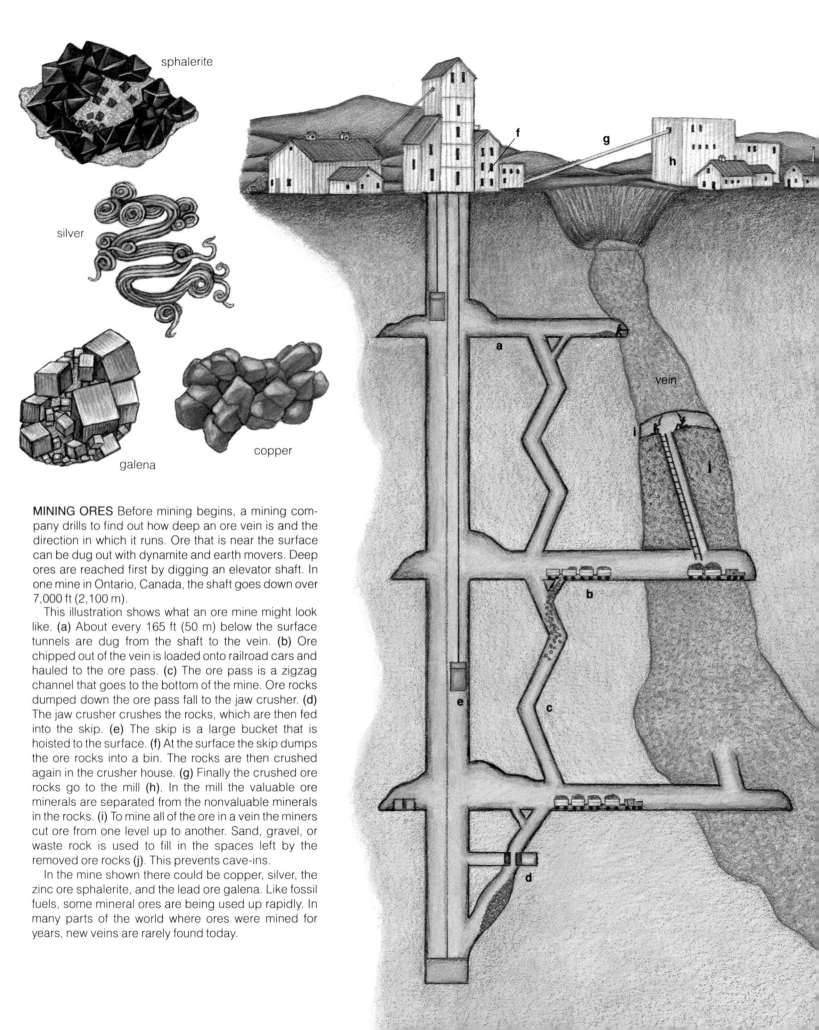

sphalerite

silver

galena

copper

MINING ORES Before mining begins, a mining company drills to find out how deep an ore vein is and the direction in which it runs. Ore that is near the surface can be dug out with dynamite and earth movers. Deep ores are reached first by digging an elevator shaft. In one mine in Ontario, Canada, the shaft goes down over 7,000 ft (2,100 m).

This illustration shows what an ore mine might look like. **(a)** About every 165 ft (50 m) below the surface tunnels are dug from the shaft to the vein. **(b)** Ore chipped out of the vein is loaded onto railroad cars and hauled to the ore pass. **(c)** The ore pass is a zigzag channel that goes to the bottom of the mine. Ore rocks dumped down the ore pass fall to the jaw crusher. **(d)** The jaw crusher crushes the rocks, which are then fed into the skip. **(e)** The skip is a large bucket that is hoisted to the surface. **(f)** At the surface the skip dumps the ore rocks into a bin. The rocks are then crushed again in the crusher house. **(g)** Finally the crushed ore rocks go to the mill **(h)**. In the mill the valuable ore minerals are separated from the nonvaluable minerals in the rocks. **(i)** To mine all of the ore in a vein the miners cut ore from one level up to another. Sand, gravel, or waste rock is used to fill in the spaces left by the removed ore rocks **(j)**. This prevents cave-ins.

In the mine shown there could be copper, silver, the zinc ore sphalerite, and the lead ore galena. Like fossil fuels, some mineral ores are being used up rapidly. In many parts of the world where ores were mined for years, new veins are rarely found today.

Water

NOTHING ON EARTH is like water. It is inside every living thing and just about everywhere else on the earth's surface. Dig deep enough and you will find water. Fly through the clouds in a plane and you are flying through water. Travel across any continent and you will reach an ocean.

Water is one of the most powerful and versatile forces on earth. As glacier ice, it sharpens mountain peaks. As rivers, it carves out canyons. As steam, it rises from volcanoes. Water wears down rocks and carries tons of sediment from the land to the ocean. Look at the damage water causes during hurricanes and floods. Douse a campfire, watch rough waves toss a ship around or a drooping plant come back to life, and you will see the power of water.

The Water Cycle

Over 97 percent of all water on earth is salty seawater. At the surface of the ocean, some seawater is always changing into water vapor, which is a gas, and entering the air. The process of changing from a liquid

The water cycle never stops. Water evaporates from the sea (a), land (b), and lakes (c) and enters the air as a gas called water vapor. Water vapor is also given off by plants (d), animals (e), erupting volcanoes (f), and some machines (g). In the air, water vapor cools to form the tiny droplets that make up clouds. Rain (h) and snow (i) from clouds fall on land and sea. Water also returns to the sea as runoff from rain (j), as groundwater (k), and as river water (l). Water locked in glacier ice (m) returns to the sea when glaciers melt (n).

into a gas is called evaporation.

When seawater evaporates, the salts in it remain in the ocean. Every day millions of gallons of water evaporate from the oceans. And as you can tell from watching puddles, strong sunlight makes water evaporate faster.

In the air water vapor can cool to form tiny water droplets. Countless numbers of these tiny droplets come together to make clouds. The process by which water changes from a gas into a liquid is called condensation.

Winds blow clouds over the land and sea. As the air

in clouds cools even more, raindrops form and fall to the earth. Rainwater is fresh water—it has no salt in it. When rain falls over the oceans, millions of gallons of water return to the sea and become salty again.

When it rains on land, some water soaks into the ground and some runs off the land into rivers, lakes, and streams. Rivers return millions of gallons of water to the sea every day, while some water in soil and lakes evaporates back into the air.

In cold places water freezes into snow and ice. About 2 percent of the earth's water is frozen in the glaciers that cover Antarctica and Greenland. When

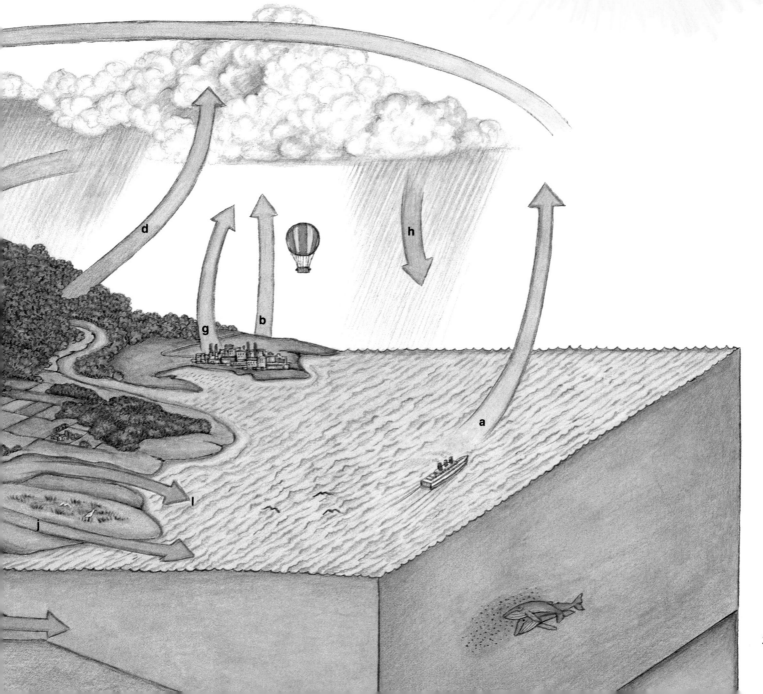

1

chamber

hot igneous rocks

2 steam

3 geyser

4

A GEYSER ERUPTS (1) Groundwater fills underground chambers and is superheated by hot, igneous rocks. (2) The superhot water expands and is pushed out of the chamber. Instantly the pressure is relieved, and some water in the chamber boils, creating steam. (3) Steam surges up to the surface, forcing out the rest of the water. (4) At the surface the geyser erupts. Steam and hot water shoot into the air. When the eruption is over, the chamber slowly refills and the process begins again. Water from geysers and mineral springs deposits minerals, such as geyserite and travertine, on the land.

mineral springs

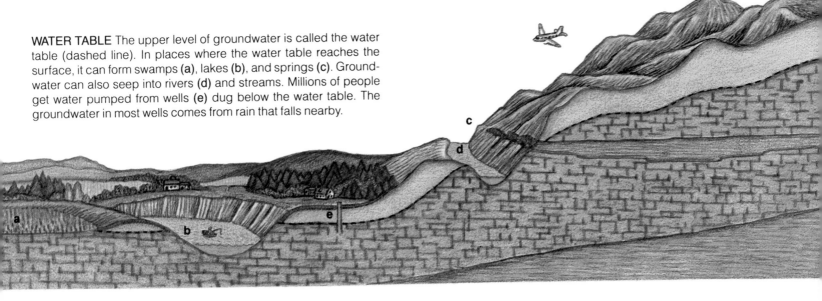

snow and glacier ice melts, even more water returns to the oceans.

All the ways in which water moves from the oceans, to the air, to the land, and back again make up the water cycle. Because of the water cycle water can be used over and over again, ensuring that there is enough for people, plants, and animals year after year.

Groundwater

First there is a rumble and a whoosh. Then steam and very hot water shoot up out of the ground. For almost five minutes they rise nearly 130 ft (39 m) into the air—higher than a 12-story building. Then the spray of water and steam dies down and disappears. It is Old Faithful, the famous geyser in Yellowstone National Park, Wyoming, erupting as it does every 70 minutes or so.

The water that shoots out of Old Faithful is ground-water. Well water is groundwater too. In fact, ground-water is all the water that collects underground. There is over 20 times more water underground than there is in all the rivers, lakes, and streams in the world.

Nearly all groundwater comes from rain and melted snow. Some of the rain that seeps into the soil is soaked up by plant roots. Most of the rest moves down to fill cracks and spaces in and between rocks. Very slowly, the water twists and turns until it comes to layers of shale or other rocks it cannot pass through. Above these rocks the water collects as groundwater. The upper level of groundwater that collects in a place is called the water table. In rainy weather or rainy seasons the water table often rises; in dry weather it may fall.

In some places the water table reaches up to the earth's surface and forms swamps, streams, lakes, and springs. In most places, though, groundwater can be reached only by digging a well.

Both well water and mountain spring water are usually cool. But the water that comes out of hot springs and geysers can be quite hot. As the illustration shows, groundwater can be heated by hot magma rocks that lie just below it in the earth's crust.

Most groundwater contains small amounts of carbon dioxide that turns it into a very weak acid, like

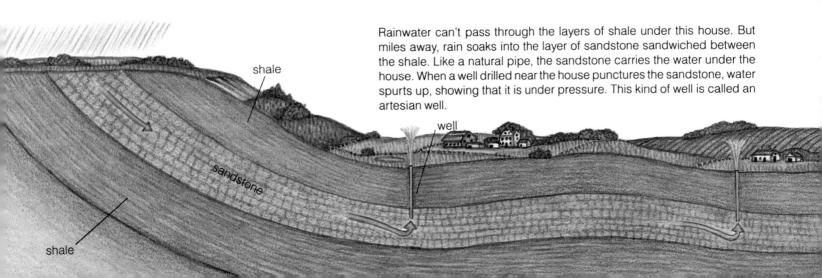

Rainwater can't pass through the layers of shale under this house. But miles away, rain soaks into the layer of sandstone sandwiched between the shale. Like a natural pipe, the sandstone carries the water under the house. When a well drilled near the house punctures the sandstone, water spurts up, showing that it is under pressure. This kind of well is called an artesian well.

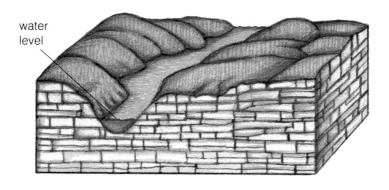

water
level

1. Groundwater seeps into the splits and cracks in layers of limestone. It dissolves the mineral calcite and carries it away.

2. Groundwater continues to dissolve away the limestone. Over time the splits and cracks grow larger and larger.

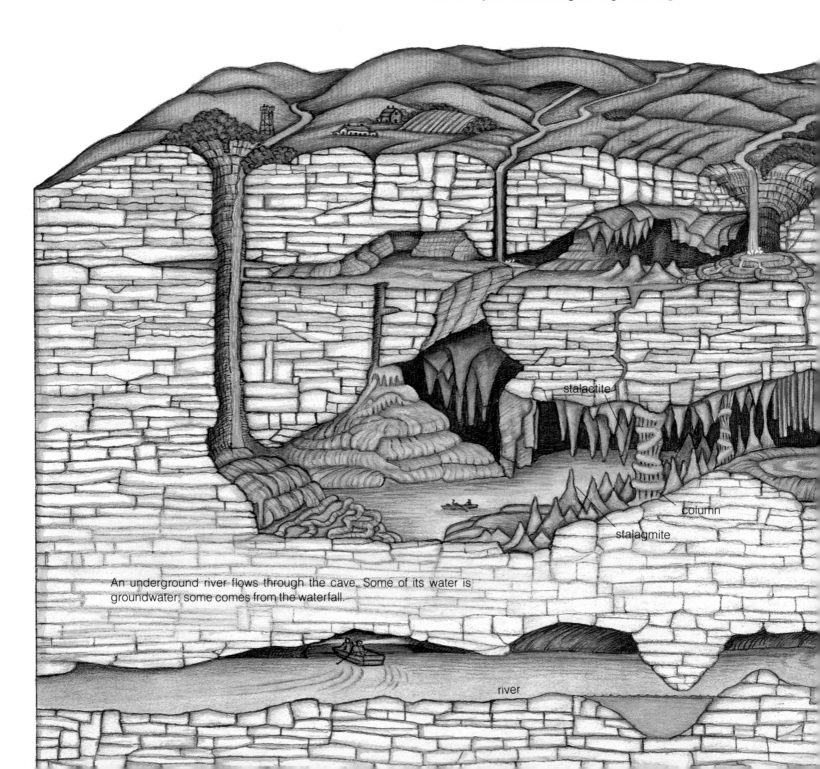

stalactite

column

stalagmite

An underground river flows through the cave. Some of its water is groundwater; some comes from the waterfall.

river

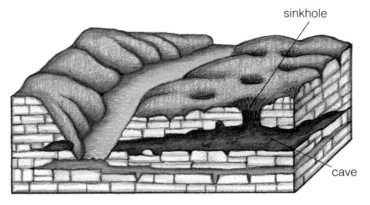

3. The level of groundwater has dropped. The splits and cracks have grown into an underground cave. A sinkhole has opened under the soil where limestone was dissolved away.

4. Water dripping from the cave's ceiling helps create stalactites and stalagmites (see text). River water disappears down the sinkhole, producing a waterfall below.

soda water. Some of the carbon dioxide is picked up in the air by falling rain, and some comes from the soil. Because groundwater is a weak acid, it can slowly dissolve certain minerals out of rocks and carry them away. For example, when groundwater seeps into the splits and cracks in limestone, it dissolves the mineral calcite. Over time, as the calcite is eaten away, the splits and cracks grow larger and larger. They form the underground tunnels and chambers found in limestone caves.

Caves and Caverns

Late one afternoon in 1902, a young cowboy in New Mexico saw millions of bats fly out of a deep pit in the ground. More curious than scared, he got a rope ladder and a lantern and climbed into the pit.

At the bottom the cowboy discovered a giant arch of rock. He noticed a wide passage and heard eerie sounds made by flying bats. As he explored, he came upon jagged ledges, curved walls, and weird, twisted pillars of rock rising from the floor into the darkness above. In the distance the cowboy heard water dripping. Suddenly he banged his head on an icicle-shaped rock and could go no farther.

Days later the cowboy returned, then brought others with him. One day, while exploring the passageways, he stumbled on an immense underground chamber, as tall as the United States Capitol Building and covering more area than a dozen football fields. The cowboy discovered what came to be known as the Big Room. It's part of the Carlsbad Caverns, and thousands of people visit it every year.

Like many caves and caverns all over the world, the Carlsbad Caverns were created by groundwater that dissolved away limestone. Once a limestone cave forms, groundwater keeps dripping from cracks in the ceiling. Each drop contains a tiny amount of dissolved calcite. In the air of the open cave some of the drops evaporate and leave behind the calcite, which hardens on the ceiling. Drop after drop adds more and more calcite as slender, hanging rock-icicles, called stalactites, slowly take shape all over the ceiling.

Groundwater drips down the sides of the stalactites and splatters on the cave floor. As these drops evaporate, blunt, rounded mounds, called stalagmites, slowly rise up toward the ceiling. Sometimes the stalactites and stalagmites meet and form a column. This is probably what the cowboy saw, as he heard the water dripping, that first day he explored the caverns.

55

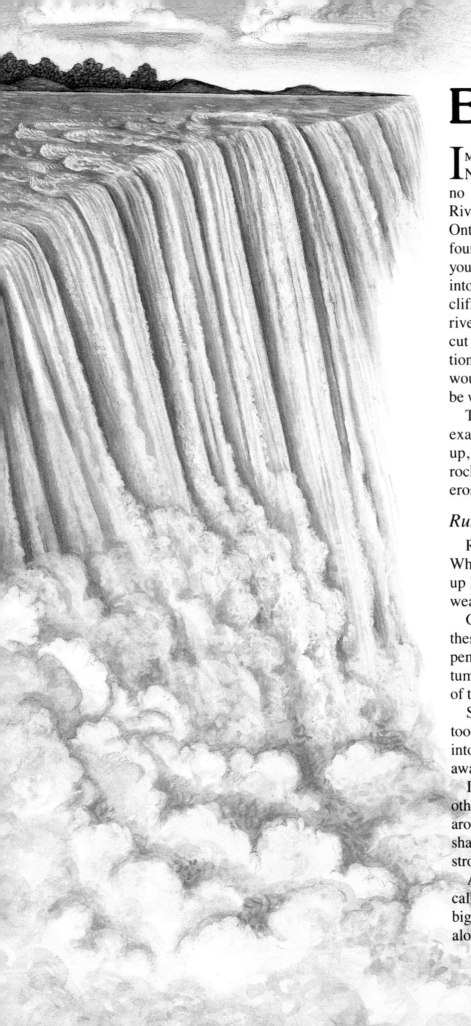

Erosion

IMAGINE IT IS 10,000 years ago. You go to where Niagara Falls is today, but you can't find it. There's no cliff, no deep gorge, only a river—the Niagara River. You follow the river for miles toward Lake Ontario. Finally you hear a thunderous roar: you have found the mighty waterfall plunging over a cliff. If you stood there long enough watching the water pound into the rocks below, you would see chunks of soft cliff rocks break off and tumble down into the swirling river waters. Little by little, you would watch the falls cut a steep-sided gorge out of the cliff (see illustration). After about 10,000 years of cutting, the gorge would be 7.5 mi (11 km) long and Niagara Falls would be where it is today.

The cutting of the gorge by the Niagara River is an example of erosion. Erosion is the process of picking up, carrying away, and depositing pieces of weathered rock. Running water, groundwater, and waves cause erosion. So do glaciers (page 62) and wind (page 66).

Running Water, Changing Land

Running water erodes the land in many ways. Whenever it rains, water washes over the land, picking up loose soil and carrying it away. Water also washes weathered rocks into rivers and streams.

Gravity pulls rivers and streams downhill. Most of these streams carry silt, clay, and sand that are suspended in the water. Pebbles and granules are rolled, tumbled, and bounced along a stream's bed—the part of the land covered by a river or stream.

Sharp edges on pebbles and granules act as cutting tools. They rub away the streambed and grind down into it. As the sharp edges are themselves chipped away, the cutting rocks become smooth and polished.

In some places a stream's flow may speed up; in other places it may slow down. If water currents whirl around, they can force cutting rocks to drill bowl-shaped potholes into the bed. If currents become very strong, they may pry rocks loose from the bed itself.

All the rocks and minerals that a stream carries are called its load. Little streams pass their loads along to bigger streams, and bigger streams pass their loads along to rivers.

Niagara Falls is one of the wonders of the natural world. It is formed by the Niagara River as it plunges over a cliff between Lake Erie and Lake Ontario. Nearly 10,000 years ago the edge of the cliff was at (a) on the map. Swirling river waters cut down into the cliff and carved out a deep gorge (b). Today (c) the gorge is about 7.5 mi (12 km) long and 300 ft (90 m) deep. Every year the rushing waters cut away another 4 ft (1.2 m) of gorge. As the edge of the cliff moves back, so do the falls. One day all of the cliff rock will be cut away and, like all falls, Niagara Falls will disappear.

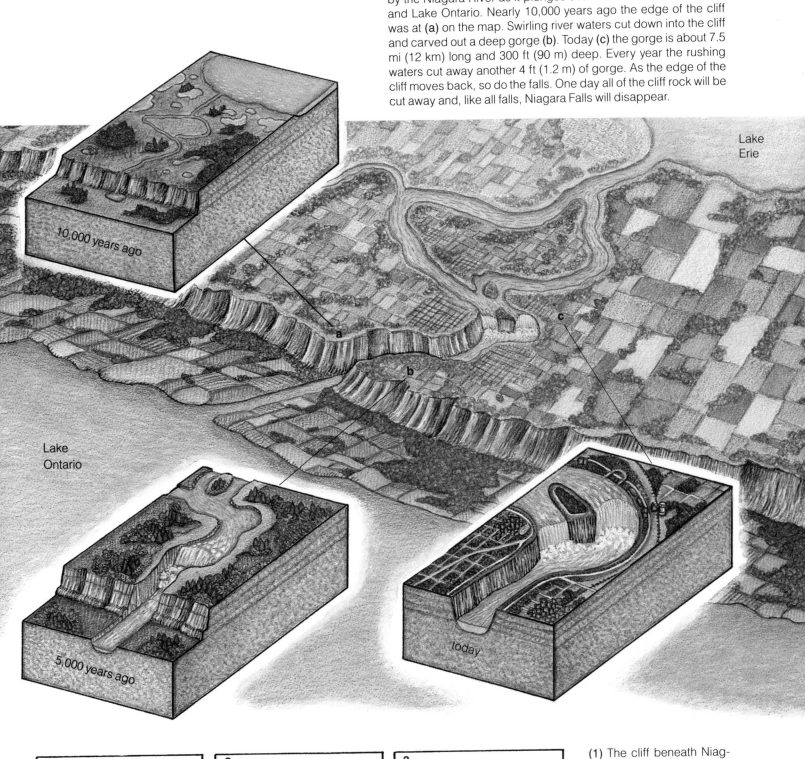

Lake Erie

10,000 years ago

5,000 years ago

Lake Ontario

today

a

b

c

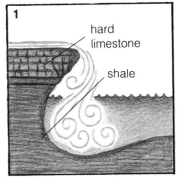

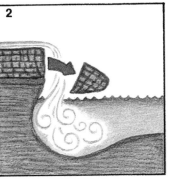

hard limestone

shale

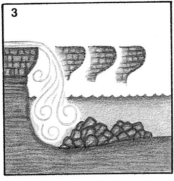

(1) The cliff beneath Niagara Falls is made of layers of hard limestone and softer shale. Plunging river waters wear away the shale. (2) When the limestone above the shale loses its support, it breaks off in blocks. (3) As each block tumbles down, Niagara Falls moves back to the new edge of the retreating cliff.

The Life of Rivers

Like everything else, rivers change as they grow older. They start off young, become mature, and sometimes reach old age. You can tell a river's stage by the way it has shaped the land under and around it.

A young river flows rapidly downhill in a fairly straight line. It is fed by just a few small streams. The load it carries cuts deeply into the rocks below and carves out a narrow, V-shaped valley. Young rivers wear away softer rock faster than harder rock. Hard rock that resists erosion can cause rapids and waterfalls to form. The Colorado River is young, even though it has been cutting through the rocks of the Grand Canyon for millions of years.

young river

waterfall

mature
river

meander

A mature river flows more slowly than a young river. It flows along the bottom of the valley it carved out when it was young. Over time the steep sides of the valley are worn down by weathering and begin to slope gently toward the river.

A mature river has cut down through the rocks that formed waterfalls and rapids, making both disappear. Most cutting now takes place from side to side. Sidecutting creates winding S-shaped loops, called meanders. Sidecutting also flattens and widens the valley floor.

When a mature river floods, it deposits silt and other sediments across the floor of its valley. The area covered by the floodwaters is called the floodplain. The Ohio and Missouri rivers are in their mature stage.

In its old age a river flows slowly and gently across its broad floodplain, away from the worn-down walls of its valley. An old river has cut down and to the sides about as much as it can. The ends of its wide loops move closer and closer together. In places an old river takes a shortcut by eroding through two of the nearly touching loop ends. Mud and silt separate the cutoff loop from the rest of the river, creating a horseshoe-shaped oxbow lake (see below). The lower part of the Mississippi River is in its old age.

Sometimes old and mature rivers become young again when the land over which they flow is lifted up (page 82). Uplifting causes a river to flow fast once more and to start downcutting a new valley with steep walls.

sea

old river

floodplain

oxbow lake

broad valley

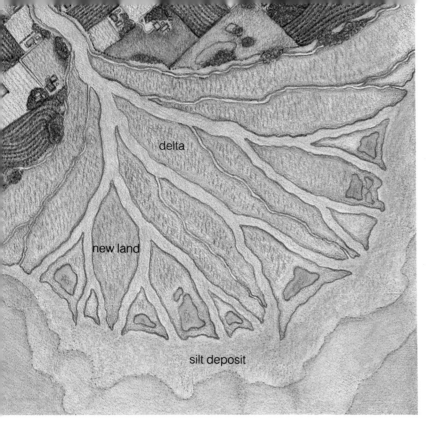

When a river flows into quiet ocean waters, it slows down. Most of the sediment it carries sinks to the sea floor. Over time the sediment piles up into a triangle-shaped delta, which can rise out of the water as new land.

A longshore current (arrow) flows parallel to the shore. It carries sand and other sediments, which it deposits when it slows down. These sediments can build up into a spit or a barrier island. Many barrier islands have formed off the east coast of the United States.

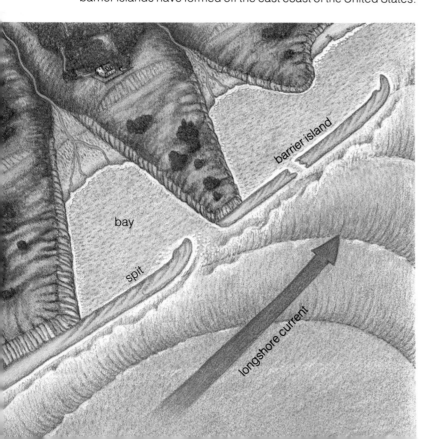

Deltas

When a river enters the sea or a lake, it slows down and starts dropping its load of sediment. At the mouths of rivers, such as the Mississippi and the Nile, the sea is relatively quiet. Dropped sediment has built up on the sea floor into great, fan-shaped deltas (see left). Other rivers have no deltas, because powerful sea currents and waves whisk the sediment away before it can build up.

Wave Erosion

Ocean waters are constantly moving. The tide rises and falls, and waves roll into shore and break. Waves can be gentle and low, but they can also smash onto the shore with tremendous force.

Ocean waves endlessly reshape rocky shores and sandy beaches. They pound into cliffs, break off pieces of rocks, and carry them back out to sea. Other waves catch the rocks and hurl them back at the base of the cliffs. Sharp edges on the rocks cut away the bottom of the cliffs, and little by little, the top of the cliff loses its support and collapses.

Cliffs take on many shapes as they are chopped away by waves. Waves form sea caves by eroding large holes in cliffs. They also form sea arches by cutting through fingers of rock that stick out into the sea.

Watch the waves breaking on shore at sandy beaches. Some deposit sand and pebbles that were brought to the ocean by rivers. Others pick up sand and pebbles and move them along the beach in a zigzag pattern. Waves carry sand and pebbles away from beaches, too. Some is caught by incoming waves and often deposited on other beaches. And some settles to the sea floor. As long as waves deposit more sand and pebbles than they carry away, the beach you are on will not be destroyed by erosion.

The greatest amount of wave erosion takes place during storms. Huge storm waves can hurl tons of water against the shore with such force that the ground shakes. During hurricanes and winter storms, raging waters rip rocks from cliffs and wash away tons of sand from beaches.

Because of the power of waves to erode the land, rocky shores and sandy beaches are some of the most changeable parts of the world we live on.

Pounding waves that break against a rocky shore erode the land. They cut away rock at the base of a sea cliff and form a notch. Rocks above the notch lose their support and fall into the water. Slowly the face of the cliff is pushed farther and farther back. As the cliff recedes, a flat platform is left behind underwater. This platform slows incoming waves, reducing their power to cut into rocks. In some places waves may hollow out a sea cave in the cliff. The four pictures at the right show how a sea arch and a stack are formed.

1

wave-cut cliff

2

sea cave

3

sea arch

sea arch

stack

stack

notch

flat platform

4

stack

(1) Waves pound against a finger of rock that extends into the sea. (2) The waves carve a large hole out of the rock. (3) The hole is cut through the rock, producing a sea arch. (4) The sea arch continues to erode. Eventually it collapses, leaving behind a stack.

61

Rivers of Ice

IN THE SWISS Jura Mountains, there is a boulder that weighs about 6 million pounds. It is made of rock that is different from the rocks around it. In fact, it is made of the kind of rock that is found on Mont Blanc, 70 mi (112 km) away. The boulder didn't roll from one mountain to the other. It was carried to Switzerland by a glacier—a slow-moving river of ice.

Glaciers form in very cold places where not all of the snow that falls in winter melts in summer. Year after year, the unmelted snow accumulates and is squeezed and pressed by the fresh snow that falls on top of it. Under pressure, the lowest snow layers melt and refreeze as rough, grainy ice similar to that in a hard-packed snowball. Over time the grainy ice turns into tough, hard glacial ice. It becomes so thick and heavy that eventually it starts to slowly move under its own weight. It is a glacier.

There are alpine glaciers and continental glaciers. The ice in both is very hard, very dense, and very cold. It erodes the land by picking up rocks and carrying them away.

Continental Glaciers

Continental glaciers form over frigid polar land areas and move out in all directions. They cover most of Greenland and Antarctica. The giant ice sheet that covers Antarctica is larger than the United States and more than 2 mi (3.2 km) thick in places.

During the earth's ice ages (page 18) continental glaciers formed and moved over vast land areas, covering everything except the peaks of very high mountains. In places the ice was so thick and heavy that land sunk under its weight. When the climate warmed, the ice melted and the land started to rise. In some parts of the world, it is still rising today.

Alpine Glaciers

Alpine glaciers form slowly on top of high mountains. As it forms, glacial ice enlarges the cracks in rocks it touches and pries weathered rocks loose. Along the bottom and side of an alpine glacier, loosened rocks become frozen in the ice. In this way a glacier scoops out a deep, steep-sided basin, or cirque. Cirques make mountain peaks sharp and jagged.

62

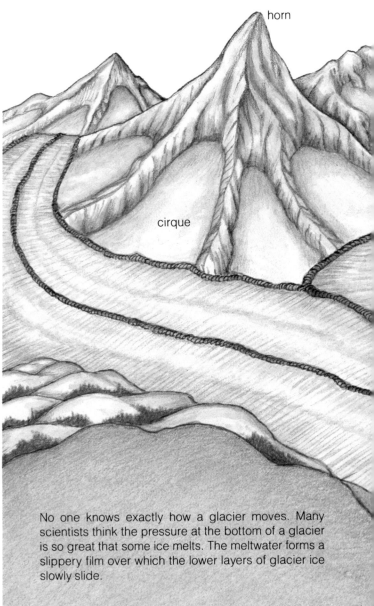

No one knows exactly how a glacier moves. Many scientists think the pressure at the bottom of a glacier is so great that some ice melts. The meltwater forms a slippery film over which the lower layers of glacier ice slowly slide.

The upper ice layers in a glacier seem to slide over the lower layers. Because the upper layers are brittle, they crack when they move. Cracks in glaciers, called crevasses, are often 100 ft (30 m) deep. Mountain climbers sometimes fall into crevasses hidden by snow.

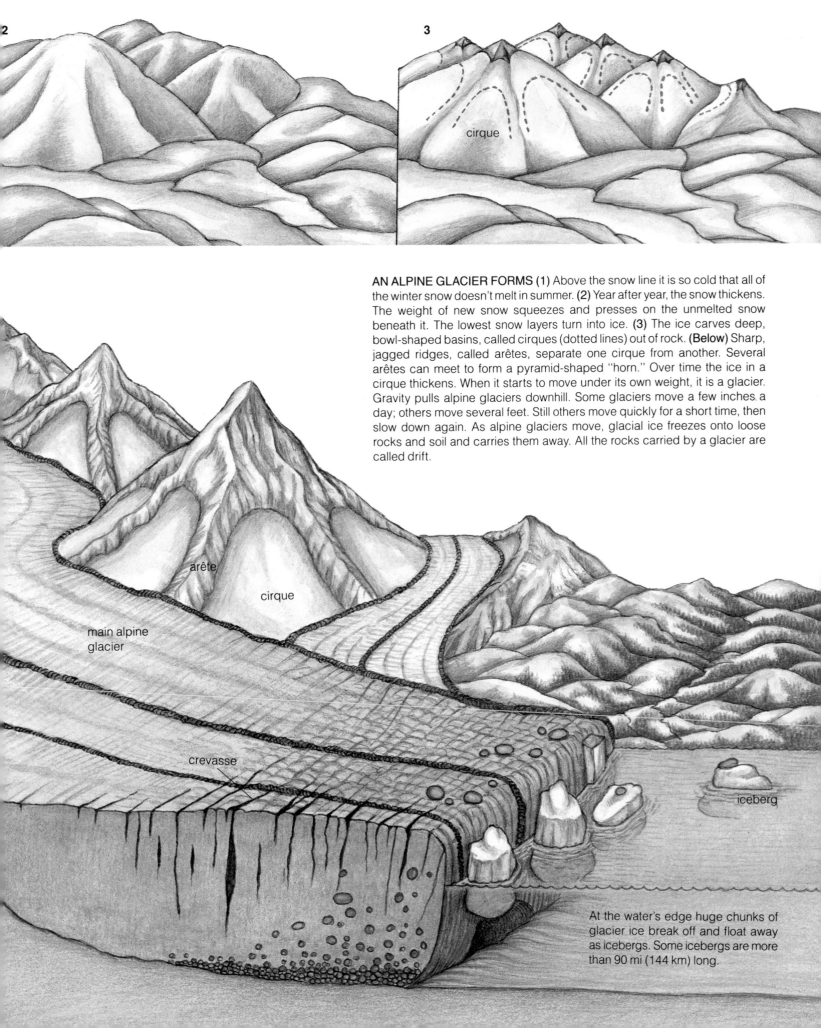

2

3

cirque

AN ALPINE GLACIER FORMS (1) Above the snow line it is so cold that all of the winter snow doesn't melt in summer. **(2)** Year after year, the snow thickens. The weight of new snow squeezes and presses on the unmelted snow beneath it. The lowest snow layers turn into ice. **(3)** The ice carves deep, bowl-shaped basins, called cirques (dotted lines) out of rock. **(Below)** Sharp, jagged ridges, called arêtes, separate one cirque from another. Several arêtes can meet to form a pyramid-shaped "horn." Over time the ice in a cirque thickens. When it starts to move under its own weight, it is a glacier. Gravity pulls alpine glaciers downhill. Some glaciers move a few inches a day; others move several feet. Still others move quickly for a short time, then slow down again. As alpine glaciers move, glacial ice freezes onto loose rocks and soil and carries them away. All the rocks carried by a glacier are called drift.

arête

cirque

main alpine glacier

crevasse

iceberg

At the water's edge huge chunks of glacier ice break off and float away as icebergs. Some icebergs are more than 90 mi (144 km) long.

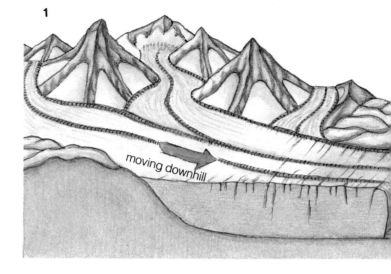

Alpine glaciers are pulled downhill by gravity. Tons of slow-moving ice scrapes and scours mountain slopes. Ice rips out loose rocks of all sizes and carries them along. Once frozen in a glacier, coarse sand, pebbles, and boulders can act like cutting tools. They scratch hard rocks the glacier slides over and gouge out deep grooves in softer rocks. At the same time fine silt frozen in the ice smoothes and polishes rocks underneath the glacier.

As glaciers creep down mountain slopes, they grind away the walls and floors of V-shaped valleys. The valleys widen, deepen, and become U-shaped.

When Glaciers Melt

Glaciers melt when they move into warmer places on land or in the sea. At the sea, huge blocks of ice break off from glaciers, float away as icebergs, and slowly melt in warmer waters. On land, melting glaciers deposit the rocks they have been carrying.

If a glacier melts as fast as it moves, the front end of the glacier stays in one place for a time. Like a conveyor belt, the ice keeps delivering rocks to the melting front of the glacier. The rocks pile up into ridges that can rise several hundred feet high. A melting continental glacier built up Long Island, New York, in this way.

If glaciers melt faster than they move, they drop a layer of rocks all over the ground. Many parts of North America and northern Europe are covered by a thick layer of dropped glacier rocks.

Millions of gallons of water flow from melting glaciers. Meltwater can carry rocks miles ahead of a glacier before depositing them. Meltwater can also carve tunnels in glaciers. When the tunnels fill with sand and gravel, they form winding ridges, called eskers.

If all the glaciers on earth melted, sea level would rise a few hundred feet, flooding most of the world's major cities.

When you travel, you can see the powerful work of glaciers in U-shaped valleys and jagged mountain peaks. The basin of a lake you drive by may have been gouged out during the last ice age. And the large boulders you see littering a field are a reminder that towering ice cliffs may once have stood there.

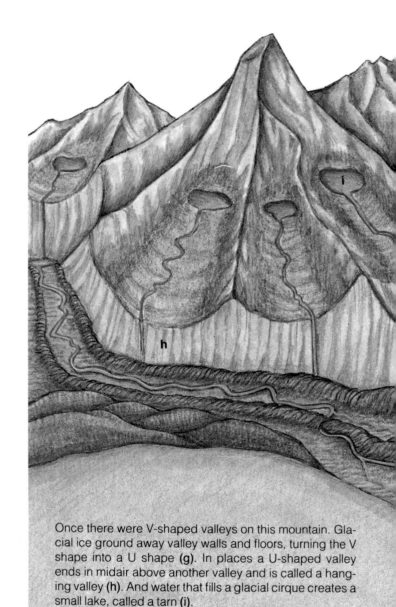

Once there were V-shaped valleys on this mountain. Glacial ice ground away valley walls and floors, turning the V shape into a U shape (g). In places a U-shaped valley ends in midair above another valley and is called a hanging valley (h). And water that fills a glacial cirque creates a small lake, called a tarn (i).

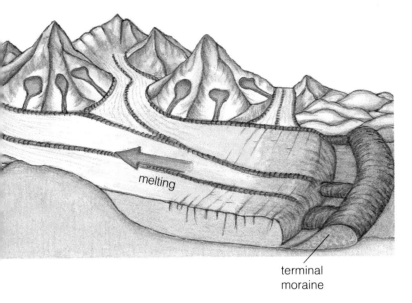

terminal
moraine

SHAPING THE LAND (1) An alpine glacier moves downhill. (2) Where the climate is warmer and drier, the glacier starts to melt. As it melts, it deposits the rocks that are trapped inside it. At the front end of the melting glacier, rocks pile up into a ridge, called a terminal moraine. The terminal moraine marks the farthest point reached by the glacier. (Below) All of the glacier ice has melted and rocks deposited by the glacier have shaped the land. The rocks have formed (a) ridges, called lateral, or side, moraines; (b) a ridge, called a medial, or middle, moraine; (c) gentle, winding hills, called eskers; (d) a small, cone-shaped mound, called a kame; (e) a thick, rolling layer of rocks, called ground moraine; and (f) oval-shaped hills, called drumlins. Bunker Hill in Boston is a very famous drumlin.

terminal
moraine

Wind and Sand

DURING THE 1930s, there was a long, dry spell on the Great Plains of the Midwest. Crops withered and there were no grasses to hold the soil together. Winds that swept across the parched farmlands lifted loose topsoil high into the atmosphere. Tons of silt and clay were blown away as dust. Some was carried by the wind as far as the Atlantic Ocean, darkening skies over many cities. So much topsoil was blown away that in places the land was lowered by several feet. Great dust storms turned parts of many states into what became known as the Dust Bowl.

The tremendous damage done in the Dust Bowl was caused by wind erosion. Most wind erosion occurs in sandy deserts, on sandy beaches, and on land that is dry most of the year.

Wind can easily lift and carry away stirred-up silt and clay. But sand is too heavy to be carried far by wind. It takes strong winds just to blow sand along the ground. And even very strong winds can't carry most

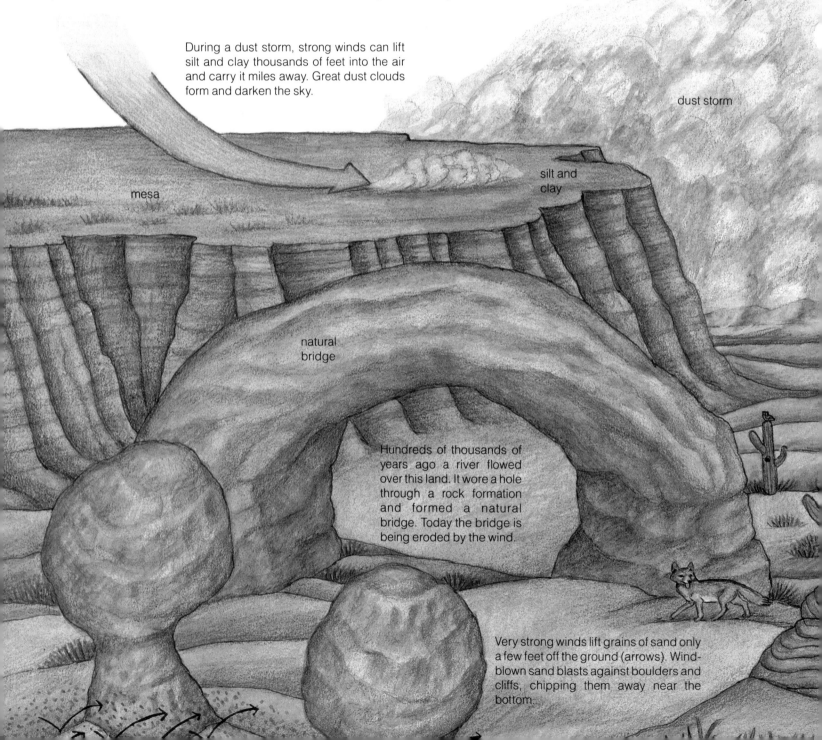

During a dust storm, strong winds can lift silt and clay thousands of feet into the air and carry it miles away. Great dust clouds form and darken the sky.

dust storm

silt and clay

mesa

natural bridge

Hundreds of thousands of years ago a river flowed over this land. It wore a hole through a rock formation and formed a natural bridge. Today the bridge is being eroded by the wind.

Very strong winds lift grains of sand only a few feet off the ground (arrows). Wind-blown sand blasts against boulders and cliffs, chipping them away near the bottom.

sand grains more than 3 ft (0.9 m) off the ground.

During windstorms sand blasts into cars, people, boulders, and other rocks. It chips away, cuts, and polishes the sides of rocks, creating sharp edges.

When the wind is slowed by rocks, bushes, fences, and other obstacles, it deposits sand in mounds and ridges called dunes. Some dunes are only a few feet high. Others, like some in the Sahara desert, grow to 700 ft (210 m) in height and form beautiful patterns as the wind moves them across the land. Traveling dunes, though, can cause problems. At times they have buried farms and towns.

Silt to Soil

Like sand, silt carried by the wind is dropped back to the ground. Over thousands of years winds have deposited silt over many areas. This silt, called loess, has formed some of the most fertile soils in the world.

In China there are loess deposits over 100 ft (30 m) thick from silt that was blown out of the Gobi Desert. The loess in Central Europe and North America came from rock powder left behind by glaciers. Some of the steep cliffs you see along the road in Iowa and Illinois are made of loess and not solid rock.

Deserts are the driest places on earth. Little rain falls in them and not enough plants grow to hold the soil together with their roots. Winds that sweep across deserts carry away loose silt and clay. Layer by layer, flat-topped mesas and buttes are lowered by wind erosion.

When winds slow down, they deposit sand in mounds, called dunes. Dunes usually form around boulders, bushes, and other obstacles that slow the wind. As a sand dune grows, it breaks the speed of the wind, causing even more sand to be deposited on it. There are two sides to a dune. The windward side faces the wind and has a gentle slope. The leeward side faces away from the wind and has a steep slope.

butte

dune

desert pavement

Below, all the sand, silt, and clay have been blown away by the wind. Pebbles and gravel, too heavy to be lifted by the wind, form a desert pavement. The rocks in the circle have been cut, pitted, and polished by wind-blown sand. They are called ventifacts.

On Good Friday, 1964, parts of Alaska shook violently. In just five minutes trees fell, land slid and sank, houses collapsed, and giant cracks opened in the ground. It was the great Alaskan earthquake, one of the most powerful ever.

Every day thousands of earthquakes occur on earth. Nearly all last less than a second and are too weak to be felt except by special scientific instruments. When major earthquakes occur, every few years, they release tremendous energy and sometimes reduce entire cities to rubble.

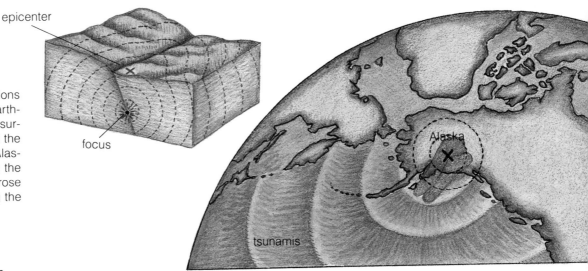

epicenter

focus

Energy waves move out in all directions from the focus—the place where an earthquake begins. The point on the earth's surface directly above the focus is called the epicenter. The epicenter of the 1964 Alaskan earthquake is shown by an X on the map. The map also shows land that rose (green) and land that fell (red) during the earthquake.

Alaska

tsunamis

Earthquakes

MARCH 27, 1964, was Good Friday and the eve of Passover. It was also the day of the great Alaskan earthquake.

It began without warning late in the afternoon. People in Anchorage heard a deep, rumbling sound, like thunder. Suddenly the earth shook. Buildings rocked back and forth, then collapsed into heaps. Like waves on the ocean, the ground rose and fell, trees toppled, water mains broke, and cars sank into giant cracks opened in the streets.

The shaking spread over land for miles. As the land moved sideways, highways were ripped apart and railroad tracks were twisted out of shape. Tons of rocks crashed down mountains as the side of one peak split off and tumbled onto a glacier.

Along the coast entire waterfronts slid into the sea. Huge oil tanks caught fire and exploded, and ships were smashed onto shore by very big harbor waves.

The violent shaking lasted less than five minutes. By the time it was over whole areas of Alaska had been lifted up a few feet and other areas had been lowered. Over 100 people were killed, thousands were left homeless, and damage totaled hundreds of millions of dollars. It was one of the mightiest earthquakes ever.

Tsunamis

Though the shaking stopped, the destruction continued, because during the earthquake parts of the sea floor had been lifted up too. Giant sea waves, called tsunamis, formed and started moving at hundreds of miles an hour. On the open ocean the waves were less than 3 ft (0.9 m) high. But by the time they reached shore, they formed towering walls of water 30 ft (9 m) high.

Tsunamis smashed into Alaskan ports, destroyed boats and buildings, swept away houses, and caused loss of life. Hours later tsunamis crashed into the coasts of British Columbia, Washington, Oregon, and California and raced across the Pacific Ocean to Hawaii and Japan.

What Causes Earthquakes

Earthquakes are caused by great blocks of rocks that suddenly snap apart. When rocks snap, they can release

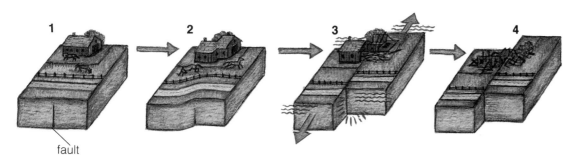

1

2

3

4

fault

(1) Beneath this land there is a break in the earth's crust, called a fault. (2) Pressure builds and builds at the fault, (p. 74), causing rocks to bend and stretch. (3) Suddenly the rocks slip and slide past each other, releasing tremendous energy that produces an earthquake. (4) The rocks spring back to their original shape. The pressure is eased, but it may rebuild.

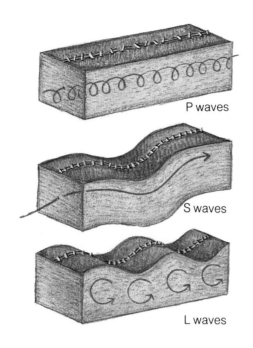

P waves

S waves

L waves

ENERGY WAVES Three kinds of energy waves are produced by an earthquake. Primary, or P, waves make rocks vibrate back and forth. They are the fastest waves and can travel through anything. Secondary, or S, waves are slower than P waves and shake rocks from side to side. Surface long waves, or L waves, are the slowest and most destructive. They can make the earth's surface rise up and down near the epicenter. Scientists measure P, S, and L energy waves using instruments called seismographs. By studying earthquake waves, scientists can tell where and when an earthquake took place and how powerful it was.

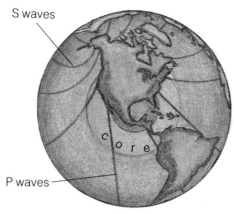

S waves

core

P waves

P waves can pass right through the earth, but S waves can't pass through the liquid part of the earth's core.

a tremendous amount of energy in a few seconds. The energy travels out in all directions from the earthquake center, or focus. It travels through surrounding rocks as seismic, or earthquake, waves.

Seismic waves can make rocks vibrate back and forth, up and down, and from side to side. Some seismic waves travel deep inside the earth. Other waves travel up along the earth's surface, causing nearly all the damage to the places where people live and work.

Faults

Many earthquakes take place along breaks in the earth's crust, called faults. At a fault rocks may be under pressure for hundreds or thousands of years. The pressure pulls and pushes the rocks, straining them. Strained rocks can only bend and stretch so far. When the pressure becomes too great, the rocks suddenly release their stored-up energy and slide past each other in opposite directions. Then they spring back to their original shapes, which helps relieve the pressure. Sometimes the rocks continue to move on and off for weeks until they readjust themselves. This movement causes small earthquakes, called aftershocks.

After an earthquake the pressure along a fault may build up again. This is what has happened along the San Andreas fault in California. In 1906 a powerful earthquake along the fault devastated San Francisco. Since then many smaller earthquakes have taken place along the same fault. Many scientists predict that within the next 100 years there will be another great earthquake in this region.

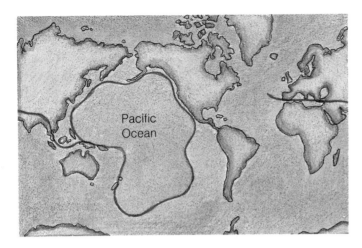

EARTHQUAKE BELTS Most earthquakes take place in two zones, called belts (red lines). One belt runs from southern Europe across Asia. The other belt runs around the edge of the Pacific Ocean. The Pacific belt is also known as the Ring of Fire because so many volcanoes occur in it.

A Million Earthquakes

Every year about one million earthquakes occur all over the world. Fewer than 20 destroy lives or property. Geologists use numbers to compare how much energy is released during different earthquakes. One set of numbers makes up the Richter scale. On that scale major earthquakes usually measure between 7.0 and 7.9. The 1964 Alaska earthquake was so strong that it measured 8.6 on the Richter scale. Most earthquakes measure less than 3.5. They are so small that they can be detected only by sensitive instruments called seismographs.

Scientists study earthquakes to try to learn how to predict them. One day they may be able to warn people hours before a major earthquake strikes.

TSUNAMIS Earthquakes on the sea floor can produce giant sea waves, called tsunamis, that possess tremendous energy. One after another tsunamis move away from the earthquake center and can speed across the ocean at more than 400 miles per hour (640 kilometers per hour).

On the open seas tsunamis are very long but not very high. Ships may hardly notice them. But as they approach shallow water, they slow down and begin to pile up. They can swell to more than 60 ft (18 m) and crash against the shore. Most earthquakes don't cause tsunamis, but those generated by the 1964 Alaskan earthquake destroyed boats, houses, harbors, and lives.

The word *tsunami* means "harbor wave." Tsunamis used to be called tidal waves but their name was changed because they are caused by earthquakes and not by the tides.

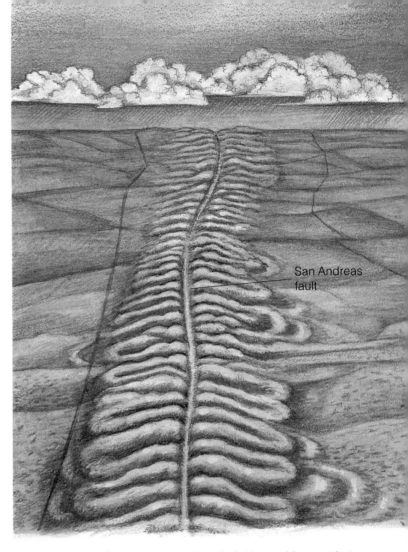

The San Andreas fault is a series of breaks in the earth's crust that runs 1,000 mi (1,600 km) through southern California. The 1906 San Francisco earthquake was caused by rocks snapping apart and moving along this fault (below). Many people fear there will soon be another major earthquake in California when the pressure along the San Andreas fault becomes too great.

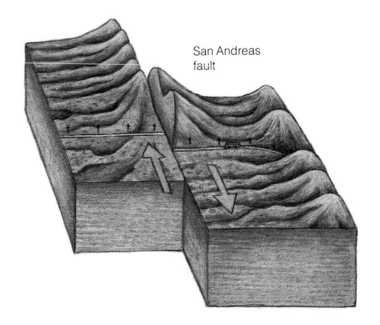

71

The Sea Floor

DURING THE TWENTIETH CENTURY people climbed to the top of Mount Everest, reached the South Pole, and walked on the moon. They probed inside living cells, split the atom, and discovered new galaxies. But what they learned about the sea floor led to a whole new way of looking at the earth.

The sea floor makes up about 71 percent of the earth's surface. For centuries people believed the ocean bottom was almost entirely flat. No one could explore deep ocean waters because of the darkness, the icy cold, and the deadly high pressure.

After World War II scientists made a map of the sea floor using special echo sounders and deep-sea cameras. The map showed that parts of the sea floor were vast, flat plains. But it also showed that in other parts there were wide valleys, miles-deep trenches, and towering mountain chains, called ridges.

Geologists studied the rocks on different parts of the sea floor and found that the oldest rocks were only

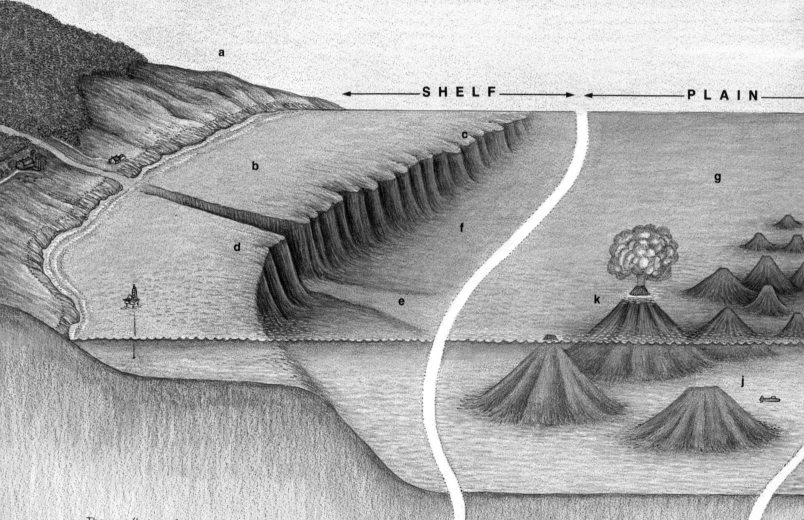

The sea floor makes up about 71 percent of the earth's surface. At the shoreline the land (a) continues under shallow water. It slopes gently down as it forms the continental shelf (b). In some places the shelf is more than 1,000 mi (1,600 km) wide. In other places it is very narrow. At the edge of the shelf the sea floor abruptly drops thousands of feet. This drop is the continental slope (c). In places, deep underwater canyons (d) cut across the shelf and slope. Some are bigger than the Grand Canyon. (e) Rivers deliver billions of tons of rock sediment into the oceans every year. The sediment covers the shelf and slope. The ocean basin (f) begins at the bottom of the slope. It has vast flat plains (g), rows of towering mountains, called ridges (h), and deep about 200 million years old. They could not understand why none of the rocks were billions of years old like some of the rocks on land. After years of further studies two scientists named Harry Hess and J. Tuzo Wilson developed a new theory about the earth called the theory of plate tectonics.

Plate Tectonics

The word *tectonics,* like the word *architect,* comes from the Greek for "builder." The theory of plate tectonics is about the building of the world we live on.

It explains why there aren't any rocks on the sea floor that are older than 200 million years. It explains how ridges form, what trenches are, and how great mountains were thrust up on land.

Because the theory of plate tectonics explains so much, most scientists believe it is correct. As you will see, geologists have already found strong evidence that supports the theory. Even so, they are trying to discover additional evidence that will make everyone accept the theory as a fact. The rest of this book is about this amazing theory.

trenches (i). Sediment covers most of the basin. Some of the sediment is mud and some forms from the teeth, bones, and shells of dead plants and animals. Undersea volcanoes, called seamounts (j), dot the flat plains. Sometimes the tops of seamounts rise above the water surface to form islands (k). Near some trenches an arc of volcanoes (l) also rises out of the sea.

The Moving Plates

THE THEORY OF PLATE TECTONICS states that the earth's crust is broken into about 20 moving plates. The plates are thick and rigid and fit together like pieces in a gigantic puzzle. Some of the plates are mostly ocean; others are made up of whole continents and parts of oceans.

All of the plates move all the time. Some move about 2 inches (5 centimeters) per year—about as fast as a fingernail grows. Others, such as the North American plate, move an inch (2.5 cm) or less in a year. In 1 million years, the North American plate moves only 15 mi (24 km) or so. Because the land you live on is part of a plate, it is moving right now. It is moving so slowly, though, that you cannot feel it.

As the plates move, their edges meet. The illustration shows where plate edges spread apart, come together, or slide past each other.

The edges of two plates slide past each other at the San Andreas fault in California. The edge of the Pacific plate moves northwest; the edge of the North American plate moves southeast. For 1,000 mi (1,600 km) along the fault, the edges scrape and grind against each other. If they become locked together, pressure builds up in the rocks. When the pressure becomes great enough to snap the rocks apart, there is an earthquake.

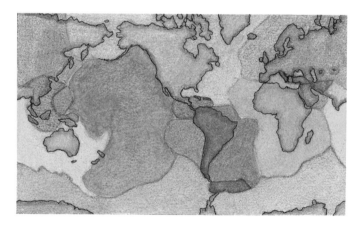

Scientists think the world we live on is broken into about 20 moving plates. Each plate is shown above in a different color. The largest is the Pacific plate, which is almost entirely ocean.

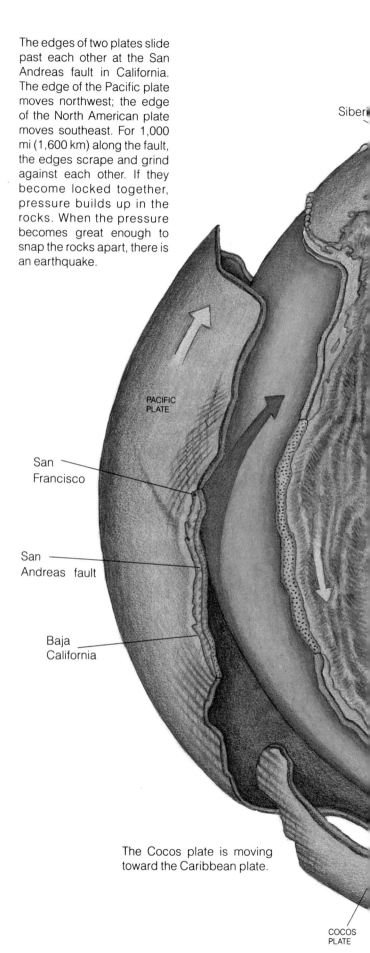

Siberi

PACIFIC PLATE

San Francisco

San Andreas fault

Baja California

The Cocos plate is moving toward the Caribbean plate.

COCOS PLATE

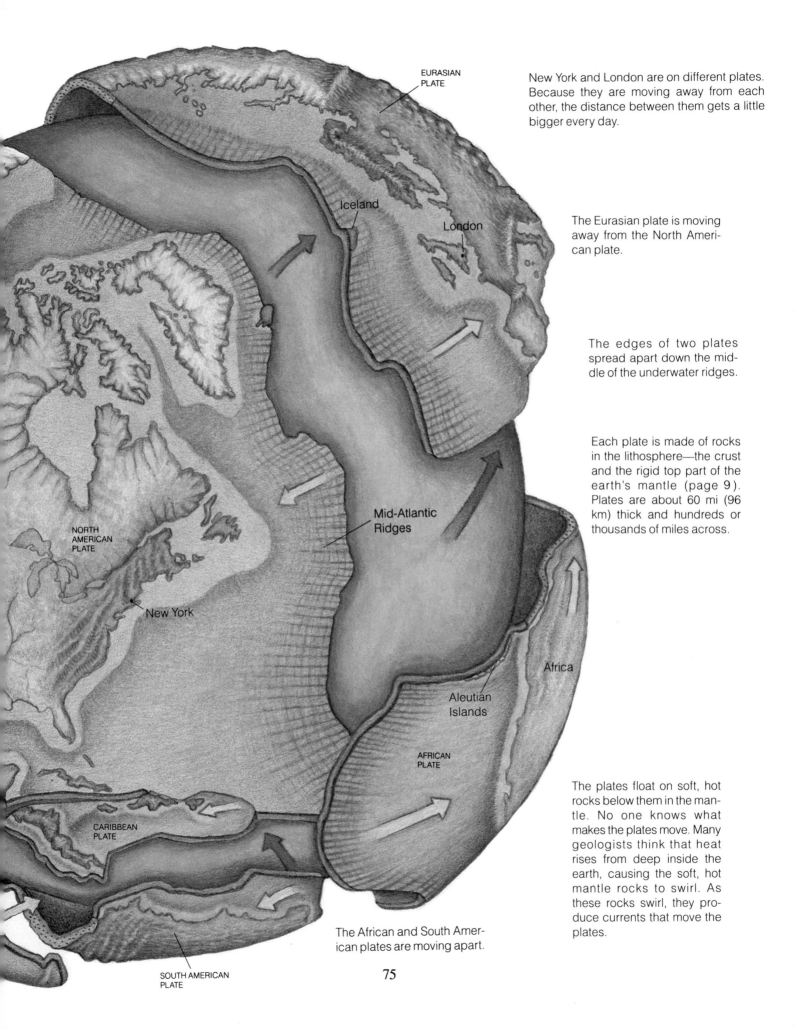

EURASIAN
PLATE

New York and London are on different plates. Because they are moving away from each other, the distance between them gets a little bigger every day.

Iceland

London

The Eurasian plate is moving away from the North American plate.

The edges of two plates spread apart down the middle of the underwater ridges.

Each plate is made of rocks in the lithosphere—the crust and the rigid top part of the earth's mantle (page 9). Plates are about 60 mi (96 km) thick and hundreds or thousands of miles across.

Mid-Atlantic Ridges

NORTH AMERICAN PLATE

New York

Africa

Aleutian Islands

AFRICAN PLATE

CARIBBEAN PLATE

The plates float on soft, hot rocks below them in the mantle. No one knows what makes the plates move. Many geologists think that heat rises from deep inside the earth, causing the soft, hot mantle rocks to swirl. As these rocks swirl, they produce currents that move the plates.

The African and South American plates are moving apart.

SOUTH AMERICAN PLATE

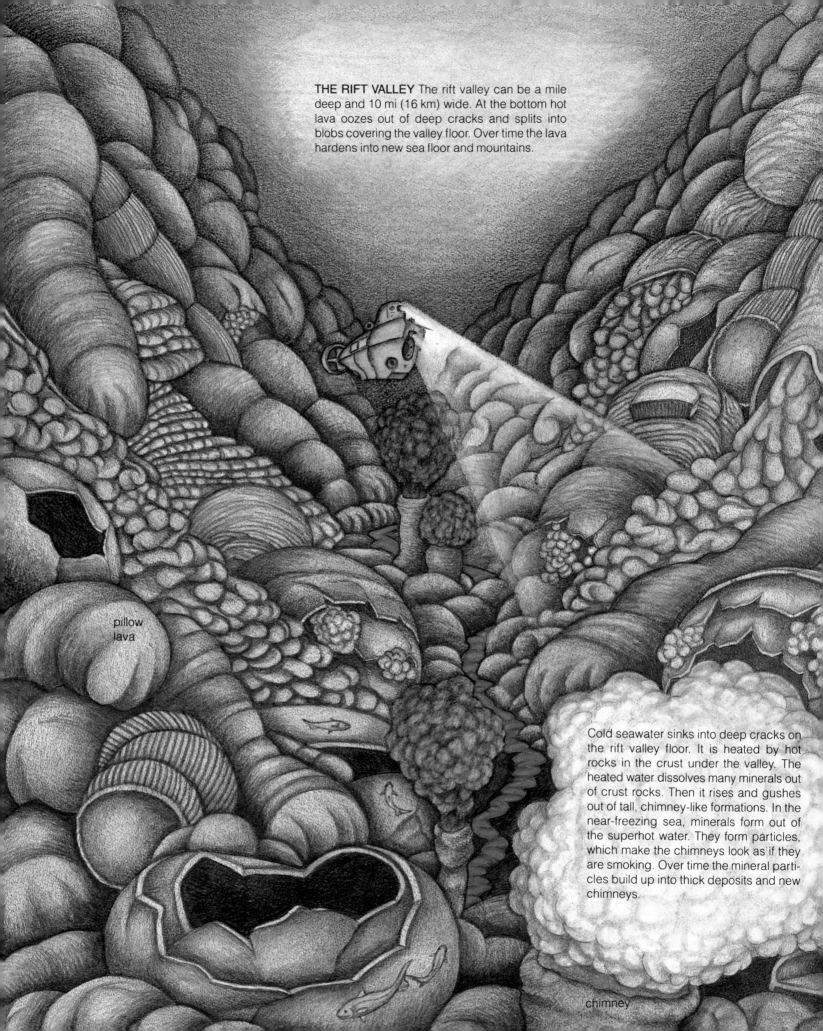

THE RIFT VALLEY The rift valley can be a mile deep and 10 mi (16 km) wide. At the bottom hot lava oozes out of deep cracks and splits into blobs covering the valley floor. Over time the lava hardens into new sea floor and mountains.

pillow lava

Cold seawater sinks into deep cracks on the rift valley floor. It is heated by hot rocks in the crust under the valley. The heated water dissolves many minerals out of crust rocks. Then it rises and gushes out of tall, chimney-like formations. In the near-freezing sea, minerals form out of the superhot water. They form particles, which make the chimneys look as if they are smoking. Over time the mineral particles build up into thick deposits and new chimneys.

chimney

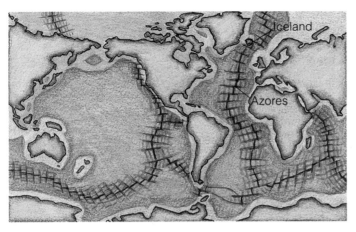

The ridges are chains of towering mountains that rise from the sea floor. They curve 40,000 mi (64,000 km) around the world and cover more than one fifth of the earth's surface. In places they are 3,000 mi (4,800 km) wide. Nearly all ridge mountains lie hidden under miles of ocean water. Iceland and the Azores, however, are really the tops of ridge mountains that rose out of the sea millions of years ago.

The Ridges

THE UNDERWATER RIDGES are the longest chain of mountains on earth. They wrap around the world like the seams on a baseball. They are made up of rows and rows of high mountains that rise from the sea floor. Some of the mountains tower more than 8,000 ft (2,400 m) high. But even such tall peaks lie hidden deep underwater.

In many parts of the oceans the ridges spread thousands of miles wide. Running down the middle there is a valley. One side of the valley is formed by the edge of a moving plate. The other side is the edge of a different moving plate. In between, at the bottom of the valley, the two plates spread apart.

As two plates spread apart, giant cracks, called rifts, open in the valley floor. Hot magma rises and slowly oozes out of the cracks. It forms strange pillow-shaped blobs of lava that stack one on top of the other. Over time the lava cools and hardens into brand-new sea floor and new mountains that become part of the moving plates. Every day, along with all the older ridge mountains, the new mountains move farther and farther away from the rift valley.

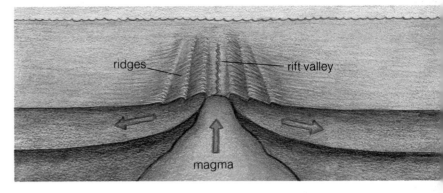

Most ridges are split down the middle by a rift valley. In the valley the edges of two plates spread apart. The spreading opens cracks, called rifts, in the valley floor. Hot magma rises under the valley, lifts up the valley floor, and oozes out of the cracks as lava. The lava hardens into new mountains of igneous rocks.

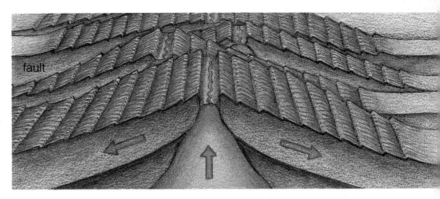

Like giant conveyor belts, the plates move the rows of ridge mountains away from each side of the valley. The ridges grow wider and wider. But once mountains move away from the lava, they can't grow higher. The newest mountains are nearest to the valley; the oldest are farthest away. Scientists measured the age of rocks taken from mountains on each side of the valley. Rocks 10 mi (16 km) away from the valley on one side were the same age as rocks 10 mi (16 km) away on the other side. Rocks 50 mi (80 km) away were millions of years older, but the same age on each side of the valley. The matching of the ages on both sides convinced many scientists that the mountains were really being moved away from the valley by the plates.

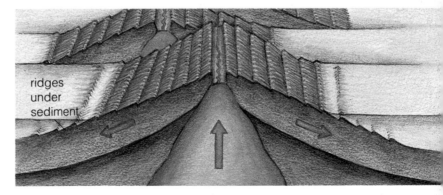

It takes about 100 million years for the new sea floor and mountains to cool completely. During this time the sea floor shrinks, gradually lowering the mountains on top of it. The mountains become covered with sediment slowly raining down from above. By the time the mountains reach the plains, they are buried under sediment.

The Trenches

IN THE RIFT VALLEYS on the bottom of the oceans, new sea floor is forming. At the same time sea floor that is millions of years old is being destroyed at the trenches.

The trenches are the deepest parts of the oceans. They occur where the edges of two plates come together. The two plates are moving toward each other.

At a trench the edge of one plate bends and dives under the other. The diving edge slowly moves down inside the earth's hot mantle. As it descends, it heats up and starts melting into magma. The magma may rise, break through the sea floor, and build an arc of island volcanoes. Or if a trench is near land, the magma may burst out of volcanoes such as Mount St. Helens.

The trenches make it impossible for us to know everything that ever happened on the earth. In fact, they have swallowed up entire chapters of the earth's story. Sea floor and crust under it that formed more than 200 million years ago have disappeared down the trenches and melted inside the earth. That's why scientists couldn't find the billion-year-old rocks they were sure had to be somewhere at the bottom of the sea.

(Below) Plate 1 and plate 2 move toward each other. At the edges of both plates there is ocean. When the plates meet, the edge of plate 2 bends and dives under plate 1, forming a trench. This process is called subduction.

The diving edge of plate 2 is stiff and cold. It slowly moves down inside the hot earth and grinds against plate 1. When plates 1 and

magma

trench

ridges

PLATE 1

PLATE 2

ma

2 lock together, pressure builds, causing weak and strong earthquakes. About 40 mi (64 km) down, the diving edge starts to melt into magma. Some of the magma may rise, break through the sea floor, and build island volcanoes. The Aleutian Islands off Alaska and the islands of Japan and the Philippines formed in this way. After about 10 million years the diving edge is hundreds of miles under the earth's surface. It keeps causing deep earthquakes until it softens and melts to become part of the mantle.

(Below right) Plate 3 and plate 4 move toward each other. At the edge of plate 3 there is ocean. At the edge of plate 4 is a continent. When the plates meet, plate 3 bends and dives under plate 4, forming a trench.

The edge of plate 4 acts like a blade. It scrapes sediments and slices of sea floor off the diving edge of plate 3. These pile up on the continental shelf, making it wider and thicker. About 40 mi (64 km) down, the diving edge starts to melt into magma. Some magma may rise, break through the surface, and build volcanoes such as Mount St. Helens. Magma that hardens inside the earth's crust thickens the continents. The stress and pressure of the diving edge as it grinds along can cause major earthquakes, such as the one that shook Mexico City in 1985.

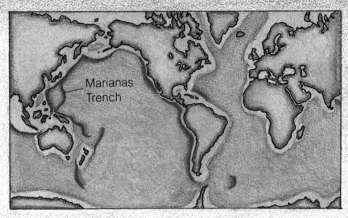

Most trenches (purple) are found in the Pacific Ocean. The deepest is the Marianas Trench, which plunges about 7 mi (11 km) below the water's surface. Many volcanoes and earthquakes occur near the trenches (see map on page 71).

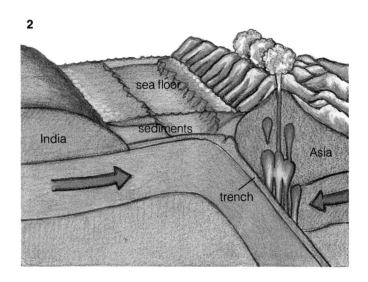

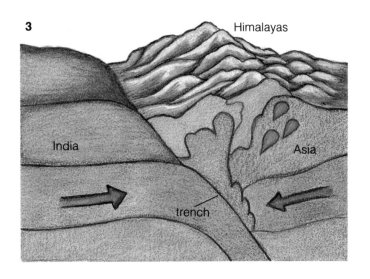

Building Mountains

NEAR THE TOP OF Mount Everest—the world's highest mountain—there are fossils of sea animals. The fossils are in sedimentary rocks that formed millions of years ago on the sea floor. How rocks and fossils from under the ocean ended up high on a mountain was once a mystery. Today that mystery is solved by the theory of plate tectonics.

Mount Everest is the best known of the Himalaya Mountains, which run along India's northern border. According to the theory, the Himalayas were built about 50 million years ago when two moving plates crashed into each other. When the crash occurred, India was at the edge of one plate, Asia at the edge of the other.

The force of the collision was tremendous. It welded India to Asia, formed the Himalaya Mountains, and raised up the Tibetan Plateau. Thick ocean sediments, trapped between India and Asia, were squeezed together by the crash, lifted out of the sea, and folded into the rising mountains. So were sedimentary rocks on slices of the sea floor that were caught between the colliding continents. The fossils in those rocks are the ones you might find if you ever climb Mount Everest (or any of the other mountains built when one plate rammed into another).

1. 80 million years ago: India and Asia are on different plates. Between them is a wide sea. India is slowly moving north toward Asia. The leading edge of India's plate bends under Asia at a trench. When it starts to melt, magma rises and builds volcanoes. 2. 50–80 million years ago: Sediments from India (orange) and from Asia (pink) build up on the sea floor. The sea narrows as the trench keeps swallowing the edge of India's plate. Like a blade, the edge of Asia's plate scrapes sediments and slices of sea floor off the diving edge. The scrapings build up into a huge wedge that rises out of the sea. 3. 40–50 million years ago: The sea has disappeared and India has reached the trench. Instead of bending under, India crashes into Asia. Sea floor and sediment are squeezed up and folded between the colliding plates. The trench closes as some of India's crust is forced under Asia and pushes up the land above it. The Himalaya Mountains and Tibetan Plateau rise miles into the sky.

4. Today: The Himalayas are the world's mightiest mountains. Most of the peaks tower more than 15,000 ft (4,500 m) above sea level. India continues to ram into Asia, as it has done for the past 50 million years. It is still pushing up the Himalayas. Each year, Mount Everest grows about 2 in (5 cm) higher.

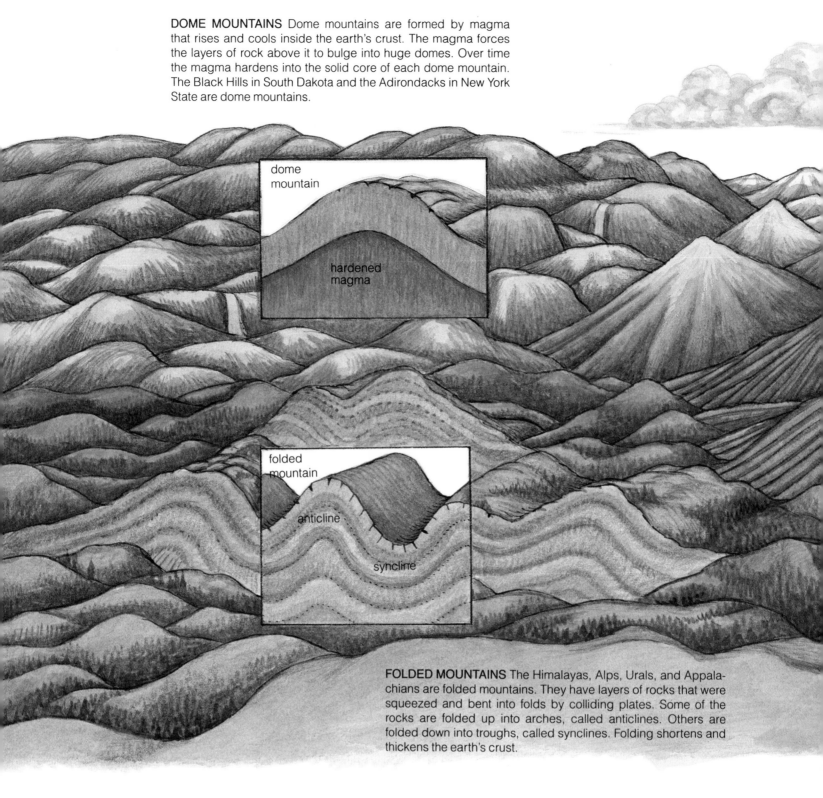

DOME MOUNTAINS Dome mountains are formed by magma that rises and cools inside the earth's crust. The magma forces the layers of rock above it to bulge into huge domes. Over time the magma hardens into the solid core of each dome mountain. The Black Hills in South Dakota and the Adirondacks in New York State are dome mountains.

dome
mountain

hardened
magma

folded
mountain

anticline

syncline

FOLDED MOUNTAINS The Himalayas, Alps, Urals, and Appalachians are folded mountains. They have layers of rocks that were squeezed and bent into folds by colliding plates. Some of the rocks are folded up into arches, called anticlines. Others are folded down into troughs, called synclines. Folding shortens and thickens the earth's crust.

Kinds of Mountains

There are four main kinds of mountains: folded, volcanic, dome, and fault-block. The illustration shows the different ways in which they are formed.

Most of the world's spectacular mountains were a result of the plates' moving. The ridges on the sea floor rise where two plates spread apart. The Andes in South America and the Cascade Range in the northwestern United States occur where the edge of one

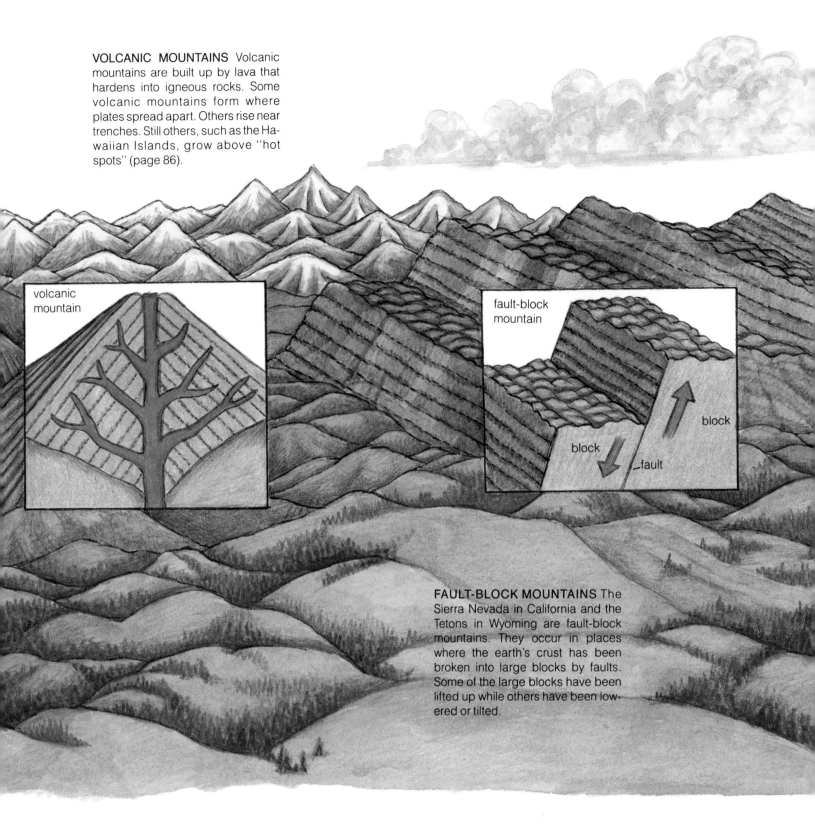

VOLCANIC MOUNTAINS Volcanic mountains are built up by lava that hardens into igneous rocks. Some volcanic mountains form where plates spread apart. Others rise near trenches. Still others, such as the Hawaiian Islands, grow above "hot spots" (page 86).

volcanic mountain

fault-block mountain

block

block

fault

FAULT-BLOCK MOUNTAINS The Sierra Nevada in California and the Tetons in Wyoming are fault-block mountains. They occur in places where the earth's crust has been broken into large blocks by faults. Some of the large blocks have been lifted up while others have been lowered or tilted.

plate dives under another. The Himalayas, Alps, and Appalachian Mountains were thrust up by the enormous force of two colliding plates.

Some mountains keep rising for millions of years. But even as they rise, they are being worn down by weathering and erosion. Imagine how many rocks you have picked up that were once part of a mountain.

In the distant future, when our most majestic mountains are completely worn away, new mountains (page 86) will be rising near the edges of the moving plates.

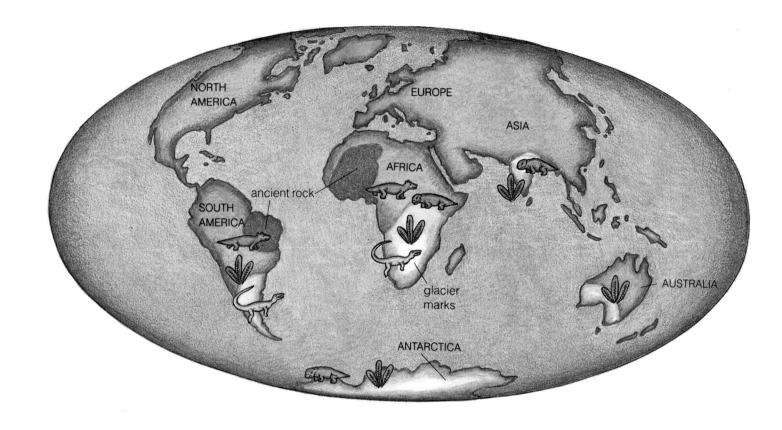

cynognathus

lystrosaurus

glossopteris

mesosaurus

THE JIGSAW PUZZLE In the 1920s, the scientist Alfred Wegener showed how all the continents could fit together like jigsaw puzzle pieces. He was certain that hundreds of millions of years ago the continents were joined as one land, which he named Pangaea. Wegener learned where certain plant and animal fossils had been discovered (pictures on the map above). He also learned where blocks of very old rocks (brown) and glacier marks (white) had been found. When he moved the continents together on paper (small map, left), the fossils, rocks, and glacier marks fit together too. Wegener believed that Pangaea broke into pieces about 200 million years ago. He said that the pieces drifted apart and eventually became the continents we live on. Since he could not explain what made the pieces move, most scientists laughed at him. Today, because of the theory of plate tectonics, many of Wegener's theories appear to have been correct.

Back in Time

MANY PEOPLE wish they could travel through time. Some would like to travel back to see dinosaurs, or watch glaciers cover Europe and North America, or explore the swampy forests where coal formed. Others would like to travel into the future to find out what the world will be like millions of years from now.

Scientists have found a way to use the moving plates like a time machine. First they study rocks and fossils on different plates. Then they trace the path of each plate back in time. Finally they draw maps of the world as it may have looked over the past 500 million years.

Some of the maps reveal that about 300 million years ago all of the continents were joined together into one supercontinent, called Pangaea. *Pangaea* comes from Greek and means "all lands."

The Supercontinent

The supercontinent Pangaea was surrounded by one vast ocean, called Panthalassa, which means "all seas." The northern half of Pangaea was the land of Laurasia. The southern half was Gondwanaland.

Pangaea lasted about 100 million years. During that time, the Ural Mountains were pushed up, glaciers covered parts of Gondwanaland, and the first dinosaurs roamed the land (see time line, page 15).

About 200 million years ago Pangaea broke into pieces. The pieces slowly drifted apart on their moving plates. Some of the pieces broke apart again. Others crashed into volcanic islands and grew larger patch by patch.

Eventually the pieces of Pangaea became the continents we live on today. Laurasia became North America, Europe, and Asia. Gondwanaland became South America, Africa, Australia, and Antarctica. India was also part of Gondwanaland. It broke away, became a continent, and moved north until it crashed into Asia.

So far, the moving plates have taken scientists back in time only half a billion years. The other four billion years of the earth's history still remain a mystery. No one knows when the first plates formed or when they started moving. And no one knows if the moving plates somehow helped life to evolve on earth.

540 million years ago

240 million years ago

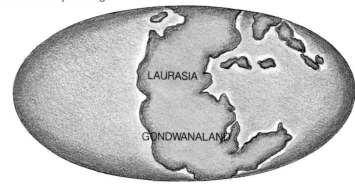

120 million years ago

60 million years ago

Into the Future

IF YOU COULD RIDE into the future on the moving plates, here's what you might see along the way: Over the next 100 million years, Africa will crash into Europe, building majestic new mountains. The Pacific plate will slice off part of southern California and carry it north until it rams into Alaska. East Africa will be pulled apart by two moving plates and a new ocean will open separating East Africa from the rest of the continent.

In about 250 million years the plates will move all of the continents together again. There will be no Atlantic or Indian oceans. Instead there will be one vast Pacific Ocean surrounding a new land of Pangaea. People will be able to bike from New York to Paris, to Cairo, to Tokyo, to Rio, and back to New York without crossing an ocean.

Geology Today

Geology is the science of the earth. It is the science of forces powerful enough to raise mountains and change the course of mighty rivers.

Just think about how those forces are working right

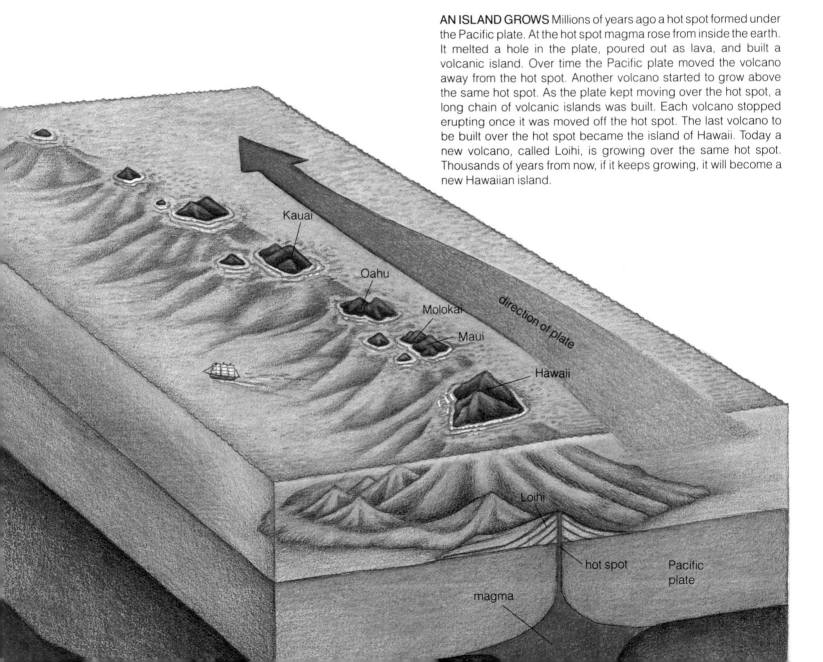

AN ISLAND GROWS Millions of years ago a hot spot formed under the Pacific plate. At the hot spot magma rose from inside the earth. It melted a hole in the plate, poured out as lava, and built a volcanic island. Over time the Pacific plate moved the volcano away from the hot spot. Another volcano started to grow above the same hot spot. As the plate kept moving over the hot spot, a long chain of volcanic islands was built. Each volcano stopped erupting once it was moved off the hot spot. The last volcano to be built over the hot spot became the island of Hawaii. Today a new volcano, called Loihi, is growing over the same hot spot. Thousands of years from now, if it keeps growing, it will become a new Hawaiian island.

Kauai

Oahu

Molokai

Maui

Hawaii

direction of plate

Loihi

hot spot

Pacific plate

magma

now! The sea floor is spreading, magma is rising, plate edges are diving and melting. Across the land rocks crack and crumble and tumble downhill. Glaciers inch along, geysers erupt, and sediment winds up in the sea. All around us, all the time, the earth's surface is changing. The world we live on will be a little different tomorrow. And the next day. And the next.

Geologists want to know even more about the way the earth works. So they map rock formations, study rivers, measure earthquakes, explore for minerals and petroleum, and even search for clues in rocks brought back from the moon. One day geologists may discover what makes the plates move, or how to tap the heat inside the earth as a source of energy everyone can use.

When astronauts first orbited our special planet, it seemed as if nothing would be more exciting than exploring space. Yet within a few years, the idea of the moving plates brought people back down to earth. It reminded us how thrilling it still is to unlock the secrets of the world we live on.

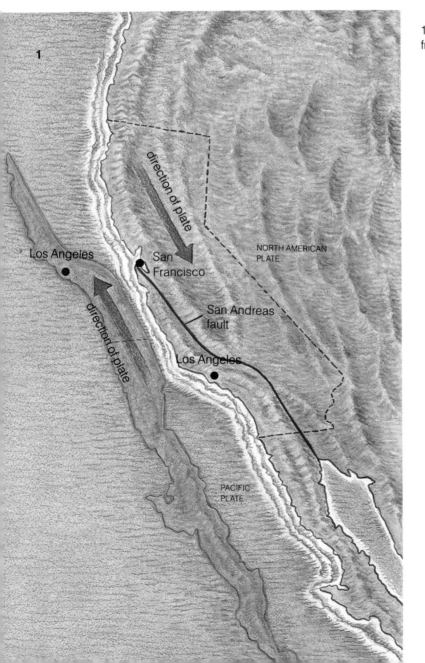

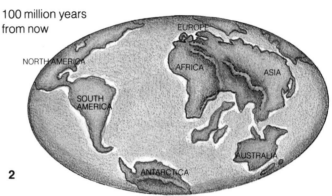

100 million years from now

1. In the future, the Pacific plate will rip Mexico, Baja, and the western part of southern California away from the San Andreas fault. The ripped land will become an island that will move north until it crashes into Alaska. Along the way the city of Los Angeles, now about 400 mi (640 km) south of San Francisco, will slide past it.

2. Earth in 100 million years: This is what the world may look like 100 million years from now. On the moving plates, Africa will crash into Europe and Australia will ram into the islands north of it. The Atlantic will become the largest ocean until new trenches form and it starts to shrink again.

3. Earth in 250 million years: Will there be a new land of Pangaea surrounded by one vast Pacific Ocean? Some geologists think so!

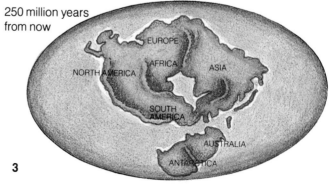

250 million years from now

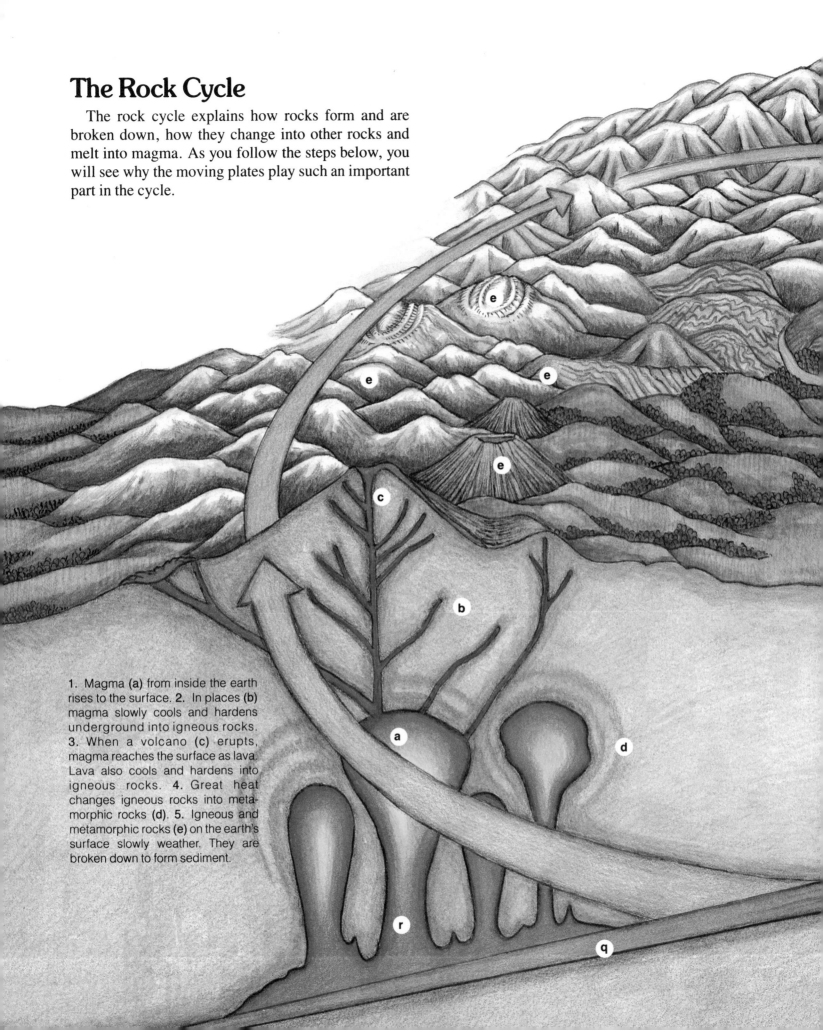

The Rock Cycle

The rock cycle explains how rocks form and are broken down, how they change into other rocks and melt into magma. As you follow the steps below, you will see why the moving plates play such an important part in the cycle.

1. Magma **(a)** from inside the earth rises to the surface. **2.** In places **(b)** magma slowly cools and hardens underground into igneous rocks. **3.** When a volcano **(c)** erupts, magma reaches the surface as lava. Lava also cools and hardens into igneous rocks. **4.** Great heat changes igneous rocks into metamorphic rocks **(d)**. **5.** Igneous and metamorphic rocks **(e)** on the earth's surface slowly weather. They are broken down to form sediment.

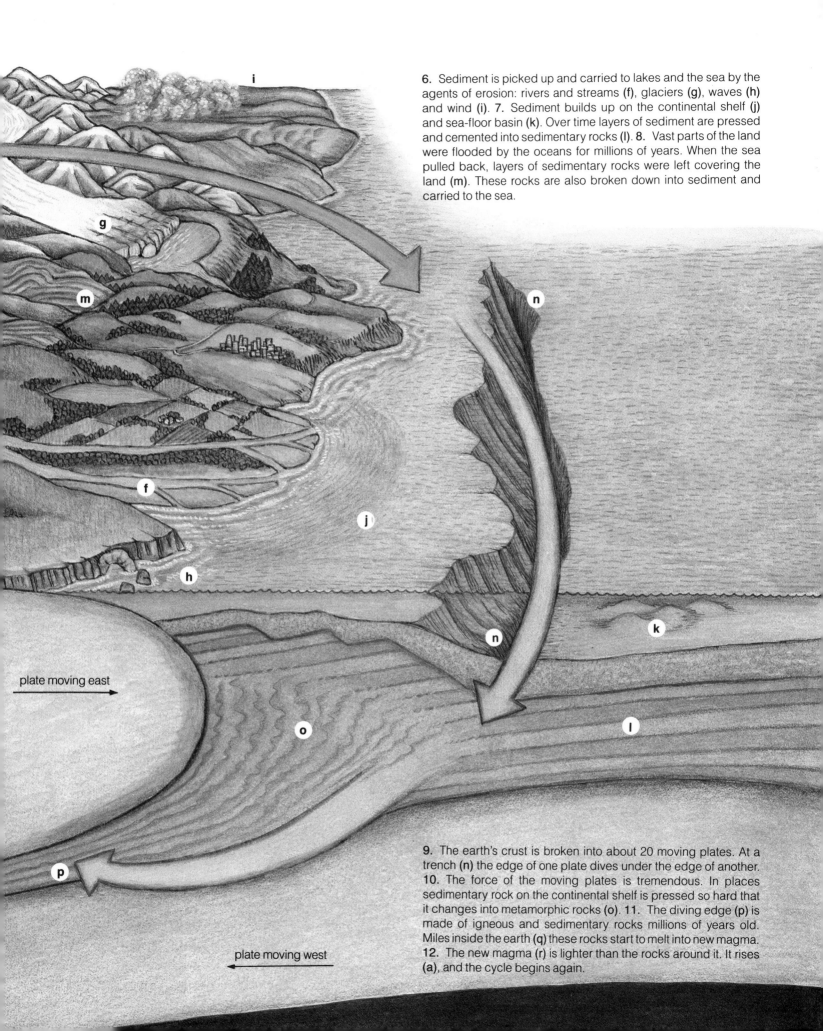

6. Sediment is picked up and carried to lakes and the sea by the agents of erosion: rivers and streams (f), glaciers (g), waves (h) and wind (i). **7.** Sediment builds up on the continental shelf (j) and sea-floor basin (k). Over time layers of sediment are pressed and cemented into sedimentary rocks (l). **8.** Vast parts of the land were flooded by the oceans for millions of years. When the sea pulled back, layers of sedimentary rocks were left covering the land (m). These rocks are also broken down into sediment and carried to the sea.

plate moving east

plate moving west

9. The earth's crust is broken into about 20 moving plates. At a trench (n) the edge of one plate dives under the edge of another. **10.** The force of the moving plates is tremendous. In places sedimentary rock on the continental shelf is pressed so hard that it changes into metamorphic rocks (o). **11.** The diving edge (p) is made of igneous and sedimentary rocks millions of years old. Miles inside the earth (q) these rocks start to melt into new magma. **12.** The new magma (r) is lighter than the rocks around it. It rises (a), and the cycle begins again.

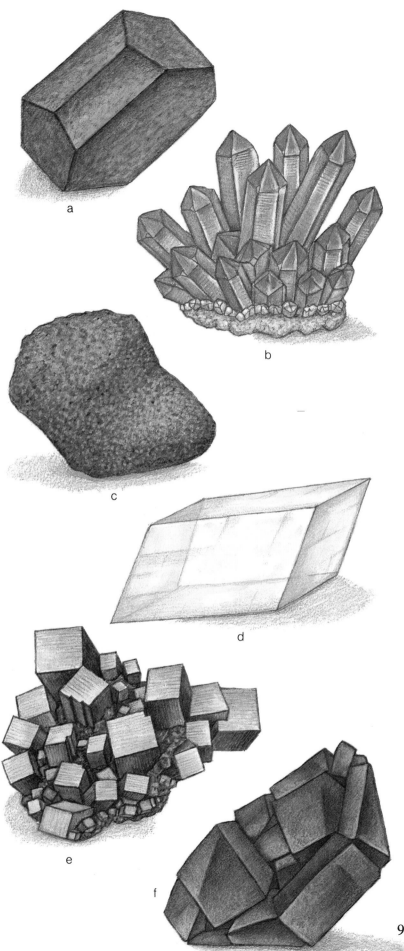

Minerals

We depend on the earth's crust for our fuels, metals, building stones—even the land on which we live. The earth's crust is made of rocks, and rocks are made of minerals.

There are about 3,000 different minerals. The mineral gold is made only of the element gold. The mineral quartz is made of the elements silicon and oxygen. Like quartz, most minerals are made of two or more elements.

Identifying Minerals

Each mineral has a set of properties that is used to identify it. These properties include color, hardness, shininess, and the way a mineral splits or breaks. Some of the ways in which these properties are used to identify minerals are illustrated on page 91.

A World of Minerals

Minerals are a vital part of our modern world. They are used in cars, homes, computers, and spacecraft. There are minerals in cement, fertilizers, wires, batteries, film, and light bulbs.

Diamond, the hardest mineral, is used in industry to cut hard materials. Quartz, a very common mineral, is used to make glass. Talc, the softest mineral, is used to make talcum powder. The "lead" in a pencil is really the mineral graphite. And the deep, rich colors of many paints come from the minerals in them.

Just a few of the earth's beautiful minerals are shown on these pages. You will find gem minerals on pages 46 and 47 and ore minerals on pages 48 and 49.

KINDS OF MINERALS Nearly all of the rocks you see every day contain minerals with oxygen and silicon in them. These minerals, called silicates, are the most common minerals found on Earth. Feldspar (a), quartz (b), and olivine (c) are silicates. So are mica (p. 25), beryl (p. 46), opal (p. 47), and garnet (p. 47).

Calcite (d), pyrite (e), and fluorite (f) are nonsilicate minerals. This means that they do not contain both silicon and oxygen. Calcite is made of calcium, carbon, and oxygen. Pyrite is made of iron and sulfur, and fluorite of calcium and fluorine. Other nonsilicate minerals are diamond (p. 47), corundum (p. 47), turquoise (p. 47), copper (p. 49), and silver (p. 49).

WHICH MINERAL IS IT? Many different tests are performed to identify minerals. Each test examines a property of minerals that can be used to tell one mineral from another. Some of the tests shown here you can perform yourself. Other tests require special laboratory equipment such as microscopes and Geiger counters.

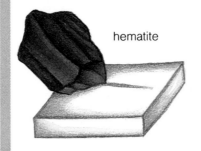
hematite

STREAK When a mineral is scraped across an unglazed tile, it often leaves a colored powder on the tile, called a streak. The color of the streak helps identify the mineral.

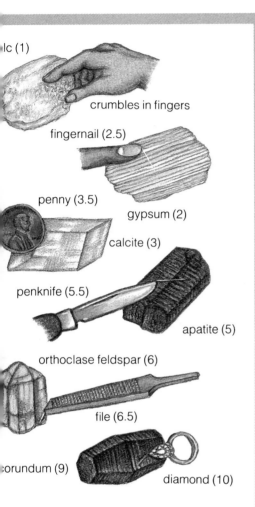
lc (1)
crumbles in fingers
fingernail (2.5)
penny (3.5)
gypsum (2)
calcite (3)
penknife (5.5)
apatite (5)
orthoclase feldspar (6)
file (6.5)
corundum (9)
diamond (10)

HARDNESS The hardness of a mineral is tested by trying to scratch it. Hardness is also tested by using a mineral to scratch other minerals or everyday objects such as a piece of glass.

Mineral hardness is measured on the Mohs scale, named for Friedrich Mohs, who devised it. The scale runs from 1 to 10 and has ten selected minerals on it. Each mineral scratches only minerals softer than it. Diamond, the hardest mineral, scratches all other minerals.

Once they are given numbers on the Mohs scale, everyday objects can be used to test minerals for hardness. A file, for instance, has a hardness of 6.5; a penny has a hardness of 3.5. If you find a mineral that can be scratched by a file but not by a penny, that mineral is softer than 6.5 and harder than 3.5.

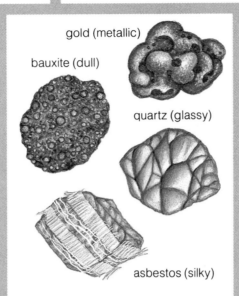
gold (metallic)
bauxite (dull)
quartz (glassy)
asbestos (silky)

LUSTER The luster, or shine, of a mineral is the way a mineral looks when it reflects light. Minerals that are shiny like metal are said to have a metallic luster. Other minerals have a dull, pearly, glassy, silky, or diamondlike luster.

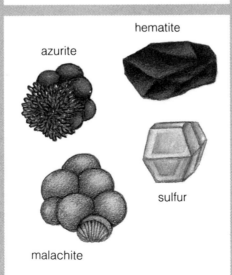
hematite
azurite
sulfur
malachite

WHAT COLOR IS IT? A mineral's color often helps to identify it, but not always. Different minerals may be the same color. Or the same mineral can occur in a variety of colors. Quartz, for instance, can be clear, purple, pink, or milky white.

CRYSTALS The atoms in most minerals join in a regular pattern to form crystals. The shape of a mineral's crystal helps to identify it. Some crystal shapes are shown here.

CLEAVAGE AND FRACTURES Cleavage and fracture tell how a mineral splits or breaks. Some minerals split, or cleave, easily along smooth, flat surfaces. The mineral mica splits into thin sheets; galena splits into little cubes. Other minerals fracture when they are broken. This means they break unevenly, forming irregular surfaces. Fractures can be rough, jagged, or splintery, or curved and shell-like.

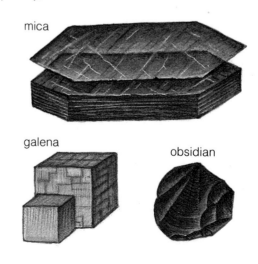
mica
galena
obsidian

When You See This...

Everywhere you go, there are clues and reminders about how the earth works. Just look around at rocks, rivers, and the shape of the land, and you can tell something about the earth's past. Many of the clues shown here tell you how the earth is changing right now. Hunting for clues can be great fun. And best of all, anyone can do it.

U-shaped valleys are a clue that the land was once covered by glaciers (page 64).

A mushroom-shaped rock is a clue that windblown sand isn't lifted far above the ground (page 66).

A stack is a clue that once there was a sea arch that was eroded by waves (page 61).

Rounded pebbles are a reminder that river waters push and roll rocks along, wearing off their corners and edges (page 56).

Layers of sedimentary rock are a clue that the land was once underwater (page 35).

Shelly limestone is a reminder that shells of dead sea animals can form sedimentary rocks (page 35).

A spring pouring out of rock means that groundwater has come to the surface (page 53).

Piles of broken rocks at the base of a cliff are a clue that weathering is taking place above (page 28).

Upfolds and downfolds often mean that rocks have been squeezed together (page 82).

A V-shaped valley was cut by a fast-moving river (page 58). It is a reminder of the power of erosion.

Index

Page numbers in *italic type* refer to material in illustrations and captions.